How to
SURVIVE
in
NORFOLK

A MANUAL FOR LONG-SUFFERING LOCALS, CRAFTY COMMUTERS, NAIVE NEWCOMERS, TESTY TOURISTS, WELL-HEELED WEEKENDERS, SOPHISTICATED SECOND-HOMERS, METROPOLITAN MISSIONARIES AND ANY OTHER OBSERVERS DRAWN TO ONE OF THE LAST GREAT OUTPOSTS OF SENSIBLE LIVING

KEITH SKIPPER

HALSGROVE

Originally published by Halsgrove, 2007
Reprinted 2008

British Library Cataloguing-in-Publication Data
A CIP record for this title is available from the British Library

ISBN 978 1 84114 654 6

HALSGROVE
Halsgrove House
Ryelands Industrial Estate
Bagley Road, Wellington
Somerset TA21 9PZ
Tel: 01823 653777
Fax: 01823 216796
email: sales@halsgrove.com
website: www.halsgrove.com

Printed in Great Britain by
The Cromwell Press Ltd, Trowbridge

Foreword

Norfolk is being invaded! But not to worry. It's all happened loads of times before. Over the years we've had Romans and Normans, Vikings and Flemms –and they all thought they knew better than us how to go about things. And they were all proved wrong.

Just now we're getting a lot of incomers who aren't accustomed to our ways. You have to wonder what they learn at school. I'm talking about people who think a cow pat is some kind of wildflower-and chiff-chaff can be cured with talc. People who reckon honeysuckle is what bees do, and wonder how we milk the chickens for cream of chicken soup. Well, this book is for them.

But it's also for people who already appreciate Norfolk but want to understand more. Because Mr Skipper knows where the bodies are buried. In fact, he probably buried a few of them himself. And you can always learn something new, can't you? Why, just last week I learned what Mrs Dace got up to with "Big" Bill Biggins after the bring-and-buy sale last Easter…You'd be amazed.

Most of all this book will show you that Norfolk -like all proper, real places –has its own flavour. And if that flavour suits your tastes then this is for you to savour with relish. Or relish with savour.

A lot of people are moving to Norfolk because it's unspoiled. This book should help make sure they don't spoil it.

Sid Kipper
Box Cottage
St Just-near-Trunch
Norfolk

DEDICATION

For all who sample the joys of Norfolk as natives, settlers, tourists and part-time missionaries. May you never take those joys for granted – or fail to protect them.

Far from the madding crowd's ignoble strife
Their silver wishes never learned to stray;
Along the cool sequestered vale of life
They kept the noiseless tenor of their way.

Thomas Gray
Elegy Written in a Country Churchyard

Naming of Parts

ACKNOWLEDGEMENTS

Renewed thanks to family and friends for encouraging me to let off more steam in the name of Norfolk culture.

Some articles, in part or whole, first appeared on my regular page, Skipper's Log, in the *Eastern Daily Press* and I am grateful to editor Peter Franzen for permission to feature them in this volume.

A sincere nod of approval towards kindred spirit Sam Llewellyn for backing the linguistic cause so colourfully in his phrasebook Yacky dar, moy bewty! , and all other writers who know the true value of local identity. They are a constant source of inspiration.

Simon Butler and his Halsgrove team have again taken the Norfolk gospel to heart and provided me with the sort of pulpit any preacher would relish.

My wife Diane used this project to carry on nurturing my embryonic skills at the computer keyboard with inestimable patience and good-natured guidance.

My technologically-sound sons Danny and Robin kindly refrained from cracking up with laughter when I happened to press the wrong button and had to call for extra support when the lady of the house was elsewhere.

It is an honour to have Sid Kipper, Norfolk's top cultural ambassador, gracing this volume with so erudite and entertaining a foreword. He needed no second invitation to do the honours despite his packed schedule and slow puncture.

Introduction

There was a time, not that long ago, when Norfolk growled triumphantly:" We don't bother the outside world – and we don't want it bothering us!"

The advent of modern marvels such as speed dating, slow networking, flush toilets, electric light and signposts pointing in roughly the right direction if the wind is in the east has opened windows that cannot be shut. Norfolk may bring out old stocks of blackout blinds from under the bed now and again, but the sun of civilisation invariably shines through.

Perhaps the odd backwater belligerent at the mercy of the moon will shake a gnarled fist or rusty pitchfork at passing fancies bound to flounder on the rocks of tried and trusted tradition.

It can also be risky for well-meaning evangelists to stray into areas where Romans, Vikings, Saxons, Danes, London celebrities and national television drama production companies came off second best.

There remains a lingering suspicion that those unfortunate enough not to be bred and born in Norfolk unerringly class themselves best suited to take the county on to bigger and better things.

Small blemishes, however, on the smiling face of togetherness as challenges and changes are handed down to the chosen people safeguarding our Promised Land in the twenty-first century.

Peaceful coexistence, not painful collision or parochial collusion, has to be the key commandment.

It is in this spirit of freshly-forged harmony that I offer my guide to survival in Norfolk, a treatise of trust to break down old barriers and build new bridges. My pedigree as a proud native, who strays beyond the county boundaries but infrequently, and then merely to remind himself of unrivalled riches left behind, will not stand in the way of common sense for a common cause.

This is a manual for long-suffering locals, crafty commuters, naive newcomers, testy tourists, well-heeled weekenders, sophisticated second-homers, metropolitan missionaries and any other observers drawn to one of the last great outposts of sensible living.

While geographical isolation has bred stronger opposition to fresh ideas than is the case in many other parts of the country, I believe the Norfolk diehard spirit is ready now to be channelled into a bold river of shared ambition and fulfilment.

It's just a matter of changing that timeworn slogan to: "If you can't beat'em... enlighten 'em!"

While reciprocal gestures could fall short of Chelsea and Mayfair apartments being opened to muddy tractor drivers once a year, I am convinced that the notorious Norfolk reserve can yield to sensitive probing and judicious appeals to a sweeter nature.

In short, Norfolk's daring to "dew diffrunt" deserves to be rewarded with a successful campaign for embracing people and interests historically in bitter conflict. The "most suspicious county in England" can earn a brand new reputation for autonomy without aggravation, independence minus impudence.

All it needs is a little humility – and a lot of humour and understanding on the part of those jammy beggars who slip past passport control or bribe border guards under the cloak of darkness.

Keith Skipper,
Cromer, 2007

LESSON ONE
BAR-ROOM BAROMETER

I cannot remember exactly who started the rumour on a dank November lunchtime in 1962. But, like all useful rumours in Norfolk, it took less than 25 years to turn into fact. Norfolk was changing fast!

My first job as a junior newspaper reporter transported me to Thetford. I called it a foreign posting as the old place shed its sleepy image and embraced the joys of overspill from London. New estates, new factories, new people, new aspirations. All rather scary for a lad weaned on a rural status quo in the middle of the county.

The Red Lion debating society enjoyed winding me up. They knew I would eagerly devour any juicy titbits tossed my way while I haunted the mean streets and generous snugs of England's fastest-growing town.

"What Thetford does today, Norfolk does tomorrow!" declared a headline-hungry voice from somewhere beyond the daily battle for smoky supremacy between Gold Flake, Park Drive and Capstan Full-Strength. I hugged my half of bitter, crumpled my crisp packet, fought back tears it would be easy to blame on the horrors of tobacco and wanted to go home to the safe world of sugar beet clamps, trundling tractors and snorting bullocks.

My partial recovery and subsequent decision to plough local media furrows for the rest of my glittering career owes much to a proud resilience (hereafter referred to as "the cussed streak") born out of that Thetford experience and a few other pub rumours, rants and reverberations.

Yes, there may have been useful discussions labelled "whither Norfolk?" in more refined quarters –council chambers and Rotary Club gatherings spring to mind –but uninhibited bar-room banter has proved a far more telling barometer when it comes to working out what's really going on in my home county..

Take the Dereham Fox and Hounds resistance movement warming up for action during the great freeze-up of 1963. There was official speculation over the likelihood of Birmingham overspill changing the character of this market town at the heart of Norfolk.

"Hands up all those who think it's a Brum ole dew!" goaded mine host Freddie Masters, a cricketing legend in that part of the world who honed his communication skills on a milk round. The pub's top-flight darts team dismissed the whole business as a load of old bull. The scheme never materialised.

Listen again to vibrant voices in the Coachmakers' Arms on the edge of Yarmouth Market Place in the summer of 1966 when World Cup football fever overflowed. Texans involved in the burgeoning offshore oil and gas industry wrote off England's chances and said we quaint locals "sure do talk funny."

Landlord Bert Price took sixpence from the till and invested in a Singing Postman number on the jukebox. We showed how we could sing funny as well.

Come with me to Beeston Ploughshare on a blossom-shaker of a 1974 spring day in my home village. I met up with a couple of old school friends anxious to prove that if only I'd paid more attention during maths lessons the world of high finance would have been my oyster. They dangled stocks and shares and inflated ambitions in front of an old farmworker cogitating as usual in the corner. He pushed back his flat cap and gently informed them that money was the root of all evil ….." an' I hev lived a fairly blearmless loife."

Stroll into the Horse and Dray on Norwich's Ber Street as a Friday teatime session ripens into a put-the-world-to-rights forum in the autumn of 1987. Enter a small but raucous party of smartly-dressed office workers clearly intent on taking the place by storm.

A gangling youth anxious to avoid being stung at the bar wandered off towards a diminutive figure hunched over the evening paper. "You got a light, Mac?" he gushed. "No," came the immediate and solemn reply. "But I hev got a dark brown overcoat."

Fast forward to the end of the twentieth century and a rare outing for a pair of mature women to the Red Lion in Cromer. They took their drinks and porky scratchings to a table near the window, made themselves comfortable and peered out to sea.

"So what are yew a'gorn ter dew ter celebrearte this here minellium, Elsie?" asked the one in the hat.

"I arnt a'gorn ter dew noffin" came the deadpan reply. "I'm a'gorn ter wait fer the next one…"

Telling little snapshots from my Norfolk album covering well over 40 years. Potent reminders of how a dash of native wit and cunning can hold back the remorseless tide of change. Inspiring examples of why cocking a snook at what many regard as inevitable ought to be cheered rather than chided.

Perfect reasons for retaining some of our pubs as places to meet and mardle rather than force them to follow the restaurant and satellite dish bandwagon.

Community survival, especially in rural areas, will hinge largely on available places and spaces for native and newcomer to exploit in the name of amiable insults. Winston Churchill, who knew all about keeping insidious forces at bay, once mused:" The only proper intoxication is conversation."

A genuine village pub can guarantee the ideal hangover.

JUST THE TICKET

Many years ago in the age of steam, a man sat in a carriage corner fast asleep on a train journey from Norwich to London. His ticket was firmly gripped between his teeth.

A gentle, rhythmic snore floated cross the compartment as the collector entered and called: "Tickets, please!" All occupants gave up their tickets – except the man in the corner.

He woke with a start and began to fumble in one pocket after another before shaking his head. After waiting impatiently for a time the collector snatched the ticket from the man's mouth and slammed the door.

A parson sitting opposite watched this incident with amused interest. He tapped our friend on the knee:

"Surely you knew it was there?"

"Yis – I wuz a'suckin' yistys's date orff."

LESSON TWO
POSITIVE NEGATIVES

As Norfolk attracts more residents, more holidaymakers, more interest, more pressures, it is vital to get certain matters right.

There are imponderables tied up with that cussed streak – when you qualify as a "local" depends more upon the folk among whom you are privileged to live rather than any fixed term of apprenticeship – but common ground can be found and tilled effectively if specific rules are heeded.

So, after earnest deliberations based on dutiful decades of Norfolk-watching in village, town and city, I offer some useful advice with which to fertilise the furrows between natives, newcomers, part-timers and holidaymakers.

These "commandments" are not cast in stone. It is up to each community to cultivate its own patch in its own way. But as the locals own the plough and the oxen used to pull it, I deem it reasonable for them to issue most of the instructions.

If the bulk of these are observed in the spirit in which they are handed down, then the roughest land can be transformed into blossoming acres. The fact they all start with "don't" ought not to infer this is a negative exercise. It is simply Norfolk care and caution being allowed full play:

▶ Don't bridle at being labelled a "furriner", "grockle" or "blow-in". It shows you have been noticed and singled out for special attention in the hope of discovering things in common. Like a sense of humour.

▶ Don't make silly jokes about Norfolk girls and the Broads. They've all been done before. In fact, these enchanting waters are the result of hard work by a good old Norfolk boy – Pete Diggins – in days before mechanical excavation.

▶ Don't buy a home near clifftops on the rugged Norfolk coast and then complain when it tumbles into the sea. Erosion is one of nature's subtle ways of stemming over-development.

➤ Don't show impatience while shopping. It's simply polite to double the time available to permit conversation with storekeepers and customers. This should be tripled in village shops where a purchase is a secondary reason for being there.

➤ Don't put on airs and graces at the first local function you attend. Watch what the natives do and follow suit as far as possible – like shouting "draw again!" if you win more than one raffle prize.

➤ Don't regard local one-way systems as a means of easing traffic flow. They are designed to put off all but the most determined from spending money in shops or clogging up the pavements.

➤ Don't forget that tractors, buses and bicycles take precedence over all other vehicles, especially in rural areas, while it is not necessary for home-grown pedestrians to look before crossing the road. They know what to expect.

➤ Don't confuse a "lazy wind" with any morning-after symptoms resulting from an excess of the local brew. It is merely a puckish breeze that prefers to go straight through you, especially on Bank Holidays at the seaside.

➤ Don't betray the fact you are a weekender through green wellies, nervous twitching, frequent glancing at your watch or puzzled looks at being spoken to by jovial locals.

➤ Don't venture into remote rural areas, especially the USA (Uther Side of Aylsham), without map and compass. First-timers should also make a will and travel with large supplies of provisions.

➤ Don't patronise locals by trying to put on a Norfolk accent. It can be managed properly only by those bred and born in the county. All other versions are made in the kingdom of Mummerzet and sold to national television and radio drama producers for a pittance.

➤ Don't move into a rural patch and then moan about crowing cockerels, church bells, septic tanks, steaming manure, wonky signposts, pot-holed lanes, reluctant tractors and wandering livestock. They give the place its charm.

▸▸   Don't argue with those who claim Norfolk is the undoubted centre of the universe. And don't mention a certain Suffolk football club in any reasoned debate about sporting prowess.

▸▸   Don't laugh if you see a farmer on a bike. Some have been feeling the pinch since rick-burning, machine-breaking and European form-filling came into fashion.

▸▸   Don't believe all the stories you hear about Black Shuck, the headless hound with fiery eyes as big as saucers. You are much more likely to spot the Hound of the Basketmeals after visiting a remote coastal pub.

▸▸   Don't automatically assume dual carriageways and other major "improvements" will make the county a better place. Back the old Norfolk slogan: "We dunt mind progress – long'as that dunt change noffin'!".

▸▸   Don't stand for any local council (or Westminster, wherever that is) if you haven't lived in Norfolk for at least five years. If you insist, expect heckling at the hustings in broad Norfolk and demands for full details of Norwich City's 1958-59 F A Cup run.

▸▸   Don't expect to discover many public toilets open along the coast if you are visiting in the summer. There's a long-running campaign to deflect more customers into souvenir shops and sea-side pubs with loos. Most patrons, it is assumed, will spend much more than a penny.

▸▸   Don't try to cook a shellduck without putting a brick in the oven along with the bird. When the brick is soft, then so is the shellduck. You don't need Delia Smith's recipe book to work that one out.

▸▸   Don't hang about if you have a secret to keep. Cancel that Norfolk residency application and return immediately to previous location.

LESSON THREE
DIALECT DELIGHTS

Norfolk's dialect, as durable and as difficult as any in the country, carries a purpose way beyond confounding newcomers, visitors and most actors searching for the authentic sound.

I regard it as a vital expression of individualism at a time when so many smothering influences are at work like a big wet blanket over any pocket of non-conformity. When it becomes apparent that those with a flair and a feeling for their local vernacular are being relegated to an ethnic minority in their own backyard, it must be time to be blatantly parochial.

More dilution may be inevitable. Judgement of character by accent seems to be growing rather than diminishing. We have been told by learned professors that folk who speak the Queen's English, technically known as Received Pronunciation, are considered to possess qualities like honesty, integrity, intelligence, ambition or even good looks. No wonder many youngsters still think it's a cause for shame to speak with a Norfolk accent!

Happily, there are enlightened forces at work to get rid of that "thick" label. Friends Of Norfolk Dialect got together in 1999 to put the battle on an official footing. A few years later they inspired a bold campaign in local schools to remind pupils (and teachers and parents) of the need to preserve and promote this precious strand of our cultural heritage.

The dialect has lasted best in more isolated areas although some speakers are "bilingual". They employ the local vernacular within their own communities, but can switch to Standard English for the benefit of outsiders or when away from their own homes. This kind of versatility will become more commonplace.

Many colourful words and expressions have disappeared with the trades and pursuits that inspired them. Horses used to rule the furrows on Norfolk farms. The old horsemen and those who worked in associated trades like the blacksmith's shop had a language all of their own.

To lump all country dialects together in one big rustic pot is a wicked affront to areas rich with individual character and respect for truly local tradition. Norfolk is not a little place wedged somewhere between Devon and Dorset as is suggested in the bulk of national drama productions on television and radio.

It is also misleading to point to an all-purpose East Anglian dialect.

There is no one brand used throughout the region – and there are always arguments as to what exactly comprises East Anglia. Rather there are many variations, not least in Norfolk itself. For example, language spoken in the Broads region is considerably different to that used around King's Lynn, which has more of an affinity with the Lincolnshire sound.

What about the old adage that Suffolk dialect is simply Norfolk set to music? Well, that's a bit of an over-simplification. It is in the southern parts of Suffolk that speakers tend to "sing", their voices rising and falling, the sentence ending on an upward note.

Here are a few helpful hints for those anxious to probe the mysteries and pleasures of Norfolk dialect. For all the grim forecasts of imminent demise over the decades it remains in remarkably good shape.

➤ Just remember….Norfolk people swallow their consonants, do strange things with their vowels and are mostly incapable of rolling an 'r' or dealing with a round 'o'.

➤ There are no firm rules for writing down dialect – and Norfolk is harder than many. "Its accents and vowel sounds are too subtle, too varied and too rich for the alphabet which suffices for the rest of the English language" said Gresham's schoolmaster Dick Bagnall-Oakeley… who wrote and spoke it with considerable success.

➤ Bernard Matthews is often seen as the archetypal Norfolk man following many years of advertising on national television. But purists claim the turkey tycoon has got it wrong as his lorries trumpet the word "Bootiful". The vast majority of Norfolk dialect enthusiasts prefer "Bew'ful", as in describing a sunny day.

➤ The dialect can vary considerably from one part of the county to another and certain words have been the subject of unjustified regional claims. Some words and expressions can be peculiar to a particular village or even to just one family. My mother called me a "want" (rhyming with "ant") for many years when I was young. I only discovered recently that this was probably a corruption of "varmint".

➤ Beware of words and expressions that might mean the opposite to what they say. "Doubt" can be used in the most peculiar manner…. "I doubt he 'oont go" really means "I'm quite certain he won't go". The word "funny" carries a different flavour in

Norfolk, meaning "extremely" as in "Thass a funny good hoss!" "Without" becomes "unless" in explanations like "He wunt go without I give him a quid to spend".

▸▸ Use of the double negative is very popular; for example an old chap on the farm complaining because he couldn't find anyone to lend a hand was heard to exclaim: "Thass the wust o' this here plearce – there ent never nobody ter help nobody wi' noffin."

▸▸ Absence of the third person singular present tense is commonplace. "He go" and "He say" are prime examples. Norfolk people make liberal use of the "historic present" as in "He see you a'comin'."

▸▸ Many words beginning with a "v" take a "w" start, willage, warmint and wittles among them. The letter can also be changed in the middle of a word, so "cultivating" becomes "cultiweartin".

▸▸ The sound of a Norfolk "a", often rendered in writing as "aa", rhymes with "air" or "care" but is well drawn out as in "Open yew that gearte, mearte, dew yew'll be tew learte."

▸▸ A long "e" can be changed into an "a", so that "beer" becomes "bare" and "three cheers" turns into "three chairs". A long "i" tends to come out as "oi" – "He wuz a'roidin' his boike". A short "e" often becomes "i" as in "Git yew out o'the way" or "I ent a'gorn hoom, not yit, I ent."

▸▸ A "road" becomes a "rood" rhyming with "wood", and "roof" is in harmony with the "woof" of a dog.

▸▸ The "h" at the beginning of a word is not usually dropped, but the "g" at the end of a word is nearly always swallowed to produce "a'sailin'" and "a'listenin'".

▸▸ Don't confuse broad Norfolk with broad Norwich, which at worst has degenerated into an adenoidal gabble. Frightening examples of such urban jargon include "Asswahreesay" (that's what he says) and "Owdsi'eegirron?" (How did the City get on?).

▸▸ Running words into one another is common practice as in "dunt paggarter orl his squit" is the colourful manner of suggesting there is little point in paying regard to all his nonsense. "Betterannerhebbin" is a memorable response to any inquiry about state of health.

TEACHER'S PET

Three Norfolk lads wanted to get on good terms with their new teacher. So they each brought her a gift.

The first boy handed over a box. She shook it and sniffed it. She knew the boy's father worked in a chocolate factory and asked if the gift was chocolate. "Yes" answered the boy.

The next boy gave her his box. Again, she shook it and sniffed it. She knew this boy's father was a florist and so asked if the gift was flowers. "Quite right," said the boy.

The third boy presented his box. The teacher again shook it and sniffed it. She knew his father worked at an off-licence and she saw the box was leaking. She tasted the fluid and asked if it was whiskey.

"No," he replied, "It's a puppy."

LESSON FOUR
BACK TO CHAUCER

It's a heartening thought that "furriners" perched precariously on the edge of Norfolk life can follow history's rich example and make telling contributions to local culture if they want to.

The dialect is made up of countless strands – Old English, Anglo-Saxon and echoes of the Low Countries for starters. Invaders from Scandinavia left plenty of words behind, probably as a penance for things they took away. Some were brought back from foreign parts by soldiers and sailors. Fishermen have done their bit as well, and so the Norfolk language has developed over the centuries.

It was that bright lad Thomas Browne, philosopher, scientist, naturalist and writer, who first noticed Norfolk had a dialect of its own in the 1600s. (He was a Londoner). Some "local" items go back to the time of Geoffrey Chaucer, surely a strong argument when doubters say the dialect is just an anachronism that ought to be swept away.

Of course, there are several Norfolk offerings that defy logical patterns or obvious derivations. Beware of these on your first visit to the village shop or pub. A playful sense of humour has led to a host of intriguing corruptions.

Here are a few of my favourite words and expressions which newcomers and visitors are likely to encounter without too much digging.

HANDY WORDS

Bishy-barney-bee – a ladybird. Norfolk historian Walter Rye was among those who thought it came from 'Been' – blessed bee. Ted Ellis, doyen of local naturalists, pointed out that ladybirds usually appear about St Barnabas' Day – that's 23 June on the old calendar. There's also support for it being a corruption of Bishop Bonners Bee. Bishop Bonner, whose cottage at Dereham near the church is now a museum, was responsible for the burning of several martyrs during the reign of Queen Mary. No doubt the fiery colours of the tiny beetles' wing cases could have led to it being given that local name. The debates continue, but it is one of the best known Norfolk dialect words.

Buskins – leather leggings or gaiters. Often worn by farm workers employed in muddy fields or in dirty jobs around the farm. They could be made of any waterproof material and fastened in several places down the side. Makeshift buskins could even take the form of old sacking wrapped around the legs and fastened with binder twine.

Cooshies or cushies – Norfolk name for sweets. It comes originally from India and was brought back home by soldiers who had served over there. A classic example of the British Empire helping out the Norfolk dialect!

Deen or dean – faint sound, usually used in the negative sense: 'he never med a deen when he come in'. It's also used in Suffolk to mean a morsel – 'there wunt a deen in Owd Muther Hubbard's cupboard'.

Dwile – floor cloth with which to clear up the little messes round the kitchen. Every Norfolk housewife had one. It comes from the Dutch word Dweyl. Don't be fooled by dwile flonking - it is a spoof sport invented in the 1960s in the Bungay area. A floor cloth is soaked in beer held in a chamber pot and then hurled at the opposing team. Such a waste of good beer!

Fourses or farses – simply an afternoon snack in the harvest field – a bit like elevenses in the morning. It was often a community effort at harvest time as the women who weren't involved in the work brought provisions to those who were – and they all sat down and enjoyed it. 'Cor blarst, I dunt half look forward to my fourses!'.

Hold-ye – still on the harvest scene, this was the call of the boy in charge of the horses drawing loads of corn sheaves. It was a warning to the man on top of the load to hold tight. Also 'howdgee' – with howd for the man on the load and gee for the horse to move on – to gee up.

Mardle – to gossip, chat at leisure. Can be used either as a verb or a noun. It also has associations with a village pond – where people met to have a chinwag. It probably comes from the old English 'moadling' – but whatever the derivation it all boils down to talking rather a lot.

Mawkin – a scarecrow or as Robert Forby put it early in the nineteenth century 'a dirty, ragged, blousy wench'. As early as the fourteenth century it was used to describe a slatternly woman. It's probably a diminutive of the names Matilda or Maude. Not to be confused with mawther – a girl or young woman.

Puckaterry – a rare old muddle, utter confusion. It is almost certainly simply a wonderful local corruption of purgatory. Someone mispronounced it one day – and another dialect word was born.

Squit – probably the best known Norfolk dialect word of all. It means a load of old nonsense – 'he talk a lot of old squit'. It is comparatively new and was originally used as a word of contempt for a diminutive person. It gradually turned into expressions like 'a lot of squit and slaver' towards the end of the nineteenth century.

Tittermatorter – a lovely word for a see-saw. You can see how it came about as you recall how 'on the teeter' meant it was tilted. In America a see-saw is called a teeter or a teeterboard. And it all dates back to the sixteenth century.

USEFUL PHRASES

All the way ter Swoffum ter dew a day's troshin' fer noffin' – Norfolk people's favourite caricature of their own dialect, delivered in an exaggerated drawl.

Are yew gorter come? – a neat trick to manage both at the same time.

Best part o' sum tyme – taking a fair while.

Betterannerhebbin – opposite to "wassanwotterwuz".

Bit slow in cummin' forrard – traditional Norfolk trait of being reluctant to seek the limelight.

Cor, blarst me! – a favourite expletive along "Well, I'll be blowed!" lines, and often used as prelude to a greeting.

Cum on in out onnit – useful advice to someone standing in the rain.

Dark over Will's mother's – signs of bad weather coming. Will's mother is not confined to Norfolk.

Dew yew keep a'troshin'! – keep at it, keep going. The Americans might say "Keep on trucking!". Troshin' is a local corruption of threshing ... sorting out the wheat from the chaff.

Ding o' the lug – customary punishment for a naughty boy – and a clip of the ear never did anyone any harm.

Dunt yew paggarter orl his squit – useful advice to someone being taking in… "I shouldn't pay any regard to all his nonsense if I were you."

Fair ter middlin' – stock response to inquiries about state of health.

Fare yew well, tergether – a fond goodbye. "Tergether" refers to all present whether singly or in a crowd. A young man was shocked when the father of his girlfriend bid them goodnight and said: "Time we all went ter bed, tergether!".

Git late earlier – the nights are pulling in.

He'yer fa'r got a dickey, bor? – traditional question from one Norfolk person to another on meeting on strange territory just to make sure their roots are genuine. It means "Has your father got a donkey, boy?". The correct reply from a fellow native is: "Yis, an' he want a fewl ter ride'im, will yew come?" meaning "Yes, and he wants a fool to ride him, will you come?"

Hev yew gotta loight, boy? – title of song performed by the Singing Postman (Allan Smethurst) in the early 1960s. Natural successor in many ways to 'he'yer fa'r got a dickey, bor?'.

Hold yew hard! – hang on a moment

Jargon – (a little cheat) what healthy Norfolk people do before breakfast – go a'jargon.

Keptathometogoataterin' – classic excuse in a note sent to a teacher by a Norfolk mother whose boy had been absent from school for several days. He was busy with the potato harvest.

Knockin' an' toppin' – the lot of the sugar beet worker before mechanisation. The beet were banged together and then the leaves sliced off.

My ole bewty – as rich a greeting or description as a Norfolk native can muster.

No, there ent none, nut fer nobody – postman's reply on being asked if he has any letters for Sunnybrook Farm. Emphatic use of negative also found in "Yew kin orl go hoom – and dunt none o'yew never come back no more."

Old Year's Night – New Year's Eve.

Rum ole dew – a very strange business.

Slow ole dry out terday – a wry summary of very wet weather.

Stand well clear o'yarself – important instructions to be followed on Bonfire Night.

Summer an' winter 'em fust – dominant characteristic of Norfolk people, especially where newcomers are concerned. Wait until you have their measure before accepting them.

Suffin' goin' abowt – Norfolk's most common ailment.

That'll larn yer! – Serves you right, my good man and let us hope the lesson has gone home!

Thrippence short of a shillin' – not quite the whole ticket. Same as "a few sticks short of a bundle."

Wossitgotterdewwi'yew? – rebuke to anyone being too inquisitive.

ON THE BALL

Boss: "You know something, Blythe, it hasn't escaped my notice that every time Norwich City have a mid-week game, for some reason you have to take your granny to the doctor's."

Blythe: "Good heavens, sir, you're right. Don't think she's faking it by any chance?"

LESSON FIVE
FUNNY FONETICS

Adialect worth keeping has to be flexible and resilient enough to put up with all sorts of irreverent treatment –and still remain largely true to its roots.

Norfolk, and Norwich in particular, has been subjected to countless juice-extracting exercises over the years, the bulk of them conducted without spite by people who know how to use informal language for healthy laughs. Naturally, a university city will spawn a truly helpful glossary or two (with an academic bonus), while that distinctive Norwich sound has been transferred successfully to the stage in recent years by local comedians, The Nimmo Twins.

Their offerings are much sharper, more calculating than the traditional rustic humour based on gentle ribbing and masterly understatement. Some find their impressions of city estate residents rather rude and unnerving, laughing at their idiosyncrasies rather than celebrating them. Perhaps the demands of an "in-your-face" television age were bound to push aside the homely village hall climate.

With no specific rules to follow in writing down words and expressions peculiar to a certain place, impromptu guides can vary radically… although much of it will become clear when they are read out loud.

It is generally agreed that Norwich is pronounced "Norridge" to rhyme with porridge. But that shouldn't stand in the way of other colourful versions like "Naaaaridge", which according to one whimsical guide doing the rounds in recent times " is in the south-east of England and was invented in 1923.It has a population of approximately 2500, of which 2438 are related to each other while the rest are classed as furriners. The city was built by Nicholas Parsons, a man of the cloth, for somewhere to keep his racing pigeons."

With that sort of helpful preamble, the "Naaaaridge" vocabulary should not be too difficult to grasp. Many a newcomer to the fine city, students included, will find precious survival rations in examples like these:

Naaaaridge Yoonyun – major Norfolk and Sri-Lankan employer.
Thangkyer - spoken at high speed, used by local shop assistants when accepting money.
Ass a jook - I'm just kidding.

Khazi – suburb on western edge of the city.
Loosetarfed - east coast fishing port.
Card - traditionally eaten with chips. Might well have been caught off Loosetarfed.
KooDee - discount shop at top of St Stephen's in the city.
Humbase - DIY store.
Fooze - electrical component on sale at Humbase.
Stoopud - term applied to very silly people.
Gatoo - sticky chocolate cake.
Footo or **foota** - get these developed at Boots.
Sproight - fizzy lemon drink.
Aryer orrite, bor?- good morning.
Aryer orrite, bor?- good afternoon.
Aryer orrite, bor?- good evening.
Loightarse - lighthouse.
Thass a bit on the huh - a bit wonky, uneven.
Tra'er - farming vehicle.
Cumbine arvista - agricultural vehicle.
Carra Rud - a place where Naaaaridge people go to watch their football team lose.
Wot yoo up to'urday?- what are you doing today?
Ci'ee - as in Naaaaridge city, a place for shopping (shaaaapin')
Noo idare - I don't have a clue.
Luvly ole jarb - excellent.
Cho – goodbye.

For me, a little volume first published in 1985 still provides amusement and enlightenment on a wider scale. And never let it be said that a Norfolk native with linguistic tendencies cannot occasionally look and listen over the county fence. It may lead to a sudden nosebleed, or leave him more befuddled than before, but the sight and sound of a few others struggling to make themselves clear does wonders for self-confidence Sam Llewellyn produced *Yackey dar moy bewty!*, a phrasebook for the regions of Britain (with Irish supplement). In this context, Norfolk had to be content with its role as part of The East rather than glory in geographical and cultural isolation on the happy road to nowhere. Nevertheless, the guide managed to catch a strong whiff of the authentic Norfolk character as well as sharing cheerful traits easily recognised in different parts of the kingdom.

The scene-setting certainly struck a telling note in every rural corner where the tourist has the audacity to harbour hope that he might be welcome:

"If you pass down any lane in the country this summer, you will eventually see the following sight. A person of pale and sweaty appearance will be sitting in a clean car, clutching a map and looking haggard. Immediately on his left, his wife or other companion will be snarling evilly. On his right, outside the car window, a person of rustic mien will be explaining in thick dialect that the map is wrong and that if it was him he wouldn't have started from here anyway.

"The driver will gape uncomprehendingly; the rustic will repeat himself some five times, his patience growing thinner. The holidaymaker (for such he is) will greet the repetitions with an increasingly sickly grin, until he drives off in despair and loses himself in the bogs and forests. Later that night he will be hit in a public house for answering 'yes' to a question whose right answer is 'no'."

An all-too-familiar picture lovingly drawn to underline a constant source of fun... a flustered visitor in the deadly clutches of a hard-to-understand local. Some of the best Norfolk yarns have them in starring roles. Should the visitor adopt a snooty manner in his dealings with this simple character, well, a sting in the tale is guaranteed.

Like this episode from the early days of motoring. A smart city gent in all the latest gear came upon a ford at the bottom of a rutted lane. He called out very haughtily to a rustic standing on the footbridge:" I say, my good man, do you think I can drive through here?"

"Wuh, yis," said the man. "Reckun yew kin drive in orrite."

So the motorist drove in, only to find himself in midstream with water halfway up the bonnet.

"What the devil do you mean telling me this is fit for a motor car? You must be an idiot!" he shouted angrily.

"Well," said the rustic gently, "I dunt know noffin'bowt motor cars, but that dunt cum noo more'n harfway up our marster's ducks."

Then, having struck a bargain with the hapless city gent, he trudged away to fetch a horse and rope. As he went he muttered to himself with a grin: "That wuz ryte what I towd him bowt drivin'in. But I dint say noffin'bowt drivin'owt agin."

Back to Mr Llewellyn's tour packed with Eastern promise. He described the region as "a land cloaked in mystery, susceptible to sea fogs, biting east winds and sudden outbursts of opera. (He must have dropped in at Aldeburgh for the festival on the Suffolk coast.) Its rolling pastures, US Air Force bases and wheat prairies (Cambridgeshire?) are inhabited by a ruggedly independent race, insensitive to extremes of temperature"

Even so, he didn't forget why he had come:" It will not escape the linguist's attention that parts of East Anglia are as close to Denmark as they are to London, and that the North Sea can be a good deal easier to travel than the A10 or A11,particularly between six and ten on Fridays and Sundays. During the Dark Ages the inhabitants of Denmark were quick to take advantage of this, rushing to and fro and leaving large chunks of their speech behind them

"Even now, experts aver that the inhabitants of Norfolk are more readily understood by the Friesian Islanders than by speakers of Standard English."

With that stirring testimonial ringing in our ears, let me rekindle that special spirit of harmonious co-existence carefully nurtured by *Yacky dar moy bewty*! a few summer chapters ago, starting with tips for travellers in darkest Norfolk:

Hilloo, bor! - excuse me!
Oi oont noo where I em - I am lost.
Blass, that int noo bledda good - oh dear.
Thass loonly hare in the Brecks - the Norfolk-Suffolk borders are a sparsely populated region.
There int noo hootil afor Brendon - there are few tourist facilities.
Yew kin cum down ours if yew want – I offer you the hospitality of my humble abode.
Dew yew tun lift - turn left.
Dew yew tun roight - turn right.
Oo dare, thass brook - oh dear, the car has broken down.
Bledda fen bilt's wore up – the fan belt is worn out.
Tike orf yar toits - remove your tights.

IN THE PUB

Droy wark, hooin bate - hoeing beet makes you thirsty.
How are yew a-gooin arn? - evening, landlord.
Bitter en yew, boy the look arn it – good evening.
Chairs - your very good health.
Bledda hill, thet ont a point - you have poured me short measure.
Yare a gooin to git wrong - you are heading for trouble.
Hey's paalitic - he is very drunk.
Will, I'm arf to wark - I must go to work.
Hey's a-gooin arter the raabuts - he's off to catch rabbits.
Long-tailed raabuts – pheasants.

AT THE SURGERY

Marnin, darkter - good morning, doctor.
Moy hend is quare - my hand is sore.
Do thet hut, bor? - any pain?

Thet bulk loike blazes - yes.
What heppen, bor?- how did it happen?
Th'owd dicka stood arnut - the donkey stood on it.
Oi'll give yer titnis jeb - this is a tetanus injection.
An' yew'll be a'dewin in a day'r soo - and you will be as right as rain.

IN THE COUNTRY

Blast, thass flet! - what flat countryside!
Noo that ent – it is not flat.
Es that a rarever? - is that a river?
Noo, thass a drine – no, it's a drain.
Hair cum the hells - we are approaching the heights of central Norfolk.
That look flet to me - looks pretty flat from here.
Thass a aptic lucian - optical illusion.
Hair cum the Brecks - we are entering the pine-clad Brecklands.
Blast, thass flet! - they seem very flat.
That ent flet, that rool - no, they are rolling.

DOMESTIC SCENE

Thow'd gel hev made a foo dumplins - my wife has made us ten dumplings.
Thow'd gel hev made sevrul dumplins - my wife has made us one hundred dumplings.
Cor ter heck - oh gosh.
Blass, thass a marster gret dumplin – what a huge dumpling.
I feel a bit peckewklier – I am feeling rather ill.
Yew're a gooin to git wrong - my wife will be offended.
Hair she cum - I hear her approaching.
Whass wrong wi thet gret haystack? – what is wrong with our guest?
He's now gone an went - he has just left suddenly.
Blass thass a rum'un - how odd.
Blass that is a rum'un - yes, indeed.
Must hev bin took quare - look, he left a dumpling on his plate.
Drog up noohow! – what bad manners!

HALF TERM

Note at the bottom of a Norfolk pupil's report: "if you won't believe half of what he says goes on at school, I won't believe half of what he says goes on a home."

LESSON SIX
THAT'S THE WAY!

One of my favourite examples of Norfolk's instant readiness to enlighten the weary traveller features a chap who calls at a remote country pub to ask the quickest way to a certain parish.

"Are you walking or driving?" queried the bluff landlord.

"I'm driving" replies the anxious traveller.

"Right," says the landlord. "That's the quickest way."

Its use and impact may depend on the size and demeanour of the person inquiring but that sort of sardonic humour acts as the perfect outrider for Norfolk's battalion of bemusing placenames on signposts often still waiting to point irate Vikings in the wrong direction.

Yes, locals love the chance to fall about in unbridled mirth as strangers tumble headlong into the same old potholes. But can they be chastised too severely for exacting some form of modest revenge for all those well-rehearsed jibes about being slow on the uptake and quick to reject any outside influences?

Perhaps some of the sting has gone out of Wymondham (pronounced Windum), Costessey (Cossey) and, most celebrated of all, Happisburgh (Hazeburrer). Even so, there's fair mileage left in the likes of Alburgh, Guist, Hautbois, Postwick and Skeyton. Beware also strange local abbreviations. Garboldisham is reduced to Garblesham and Hunworth to Hunny by more puckish remnants of the indigenous population. Some still talk fondly of Hindol. They are referring to Hindolveston. Check carefully before seeking information about Ingoldisthorpe. This is another one melted down with the gold extracted to leave Inglesthorpe.

Norfolk's pleasure in "dewin' diffrunt" gives Gillingham a hard 'G' unlike its much larger Kent counterpart. It remains a matter of considerable amazement – and amusement – that little Postwick, near Norwich, glories in really being Pozzick. Guist should come out as Guyst and Salle, with its wonderful church, is pronounced Sorl.

As you study the following list of Norfolk placenames where the pronunciation is different from the spelling, bear in mind there could well be more than one local corruption or shortening. There are bound to be a few good arguments left unresolved. Only join in when you are sure of your ground. In some cases, older residents are best judges of the proper way to pronounce the name of the place where they live.

Nevertheless, this remains fertile soil for winding up the furriners and there's no guarantee that a rustic sage will resist obvious temptation to assert a subtle sort of authority on his own midden:

"Excuse me, my good man, but which road should I take to Happysberg?"

"Blarst, yew kin tearke enny wun yew like – they dunt berlong ter me."

Acle	Ayccull or Earcull (say quickly)
Alburgh	Arburrer
Alby	Orlby
Ashmanhaugh	Ashmanorr
Aylmerton	Elmerton
Aylsham	Elsham
Barwick	Barrick (near Docking)
Bawburgh	Borber
Bawdeswell	Bordswell
Beighton	Bayten
Belaugh	Beloe or Beeler (near Wroxham)
Blofield	Bloofield
Burgh	Burrer (near Aylsham)
Burgh Castle	Burrer Castle
Bergh Apton	Berrer Apton or Burg Apton (often made into one word)
Bylaugh	Beloe or Beeler (near East Dereham)
Calthorpe	Colthorpe (near Aylsham)
Cley	Clay or Cly (support for both among locals, but mainly Cly)
Colney	Coney
Coltishall	Coltshull
Costessey	Cossey
Cromer	Croomer
Dereham	Deerum (East and West)
Deopham	Deephum (some supporters for Deefum)
Dersingham	Darsinum
Earsham	Errshum
Elmham	Ellam
Fakenham	Fakenum (first part to rhyme with 'bake') or Fearknum
Field Dalling	Field Dorlin' (often turned into one word)
Fleggburgh	Fleggburrer

Forncett	Fonsett
Foulsham	Foalshum
Fulmodestone	Fullmuston
Garboldisham	Garblesham
Garvestone	Garvestun or Garston
Gillingham	with a hard 'G' (near Beccles)
Guist	Guyst
Happisburgh	Hazeburrer
Hardingham	Hardnum
Hargham	Harfum (near Attleborough)
Hautbois	Hobbis or Hobbies (Little and Great)
Haveringland	Haverland
Helhoughton	Hellowton
Heydon	Haydun
Hilgay	Hilgy
Hindolveston	Hildosten or, more locally, Hindol
Hindringham	Hindrenum
Holme Hale	Hoom Hale
Holme	Hollem (the 'l' is sounded)
Honing	Hooning (don't confuse with Horning)
Honingham	Hunningum
Hoveton	Hofton
Hunstanton	Hunstan
Hunworth	Hunny (a local delight to make it sticky for strangers!)
Ingoldisthorpe	Inglesthorpe
Itteringham	Ittrenhum
Keswick	Kezzick
Letheringsett	Larinsett
Lyng	Ling
Mattishall	Mattsull
Mautby	Morby
Mundesley	Munnsley
Narborough	Narbrer
Neatishead	Neatsud
Northrepps	Nordrupps (most colourful local corruption)
Norwich	Norridge (to rhyme with porridge)
Ovington	Ovinton ('o' as in hover)
Palling	Porlin'
Postwick	Pozzick

Poringland	Porland
Potter Heigham	Potter Hayam
Pudding Norton	Pudnorton (turned into one word)
Quarles	Kworles (near Wells)
Raveningham	Raningham
Reepham	Reefum
Reymerston	Remerstun
Rougham	Ruffam
Roughton	Rowton ('row' as in cow)
Runhall	Runnell
Rushall	Rewshall
Ryburgh	Ryburrer (Great and Little)
Salhouse	Sallus (don't confuse with Salthouse)
Salle	Sorl
Scottow	Scotter
Scoulton	Scowton
Shotesham	Shottsum
Sisland	Sizzland
Skeyton	Skytun
Snettisham	Snettsum
Southrepps	Sudrupps (another colourful local version)
Stanhoe	Stanner
Stiffkey	Stewkey (usually in association with 'Stewkey Blues' –cockles)
Stody	Study
Suton	Sewton (near Wymondham. Don't confuse with Sutton)
Swafield	Swayfield
Swaffham	Swoffum
Swardeston	Swordstun
Tacolneston	Tackleston
Tasburgh	Taysburrer or Tearsburrer
Taverham	Tayverum or Tearverum
Thursford	Tharsfud
Thwaite	Twait
Tittleshall	Tittershull
Tivetshall	Tivetsull
Trowse	Troose (but open to debate!)
Walcott	Wolcutt
Warham	Worrum
Walsham	Wolshum (North and South)

Watton	Wottun
Weybourne	Webbun
Wheatacre	Witteker (near Beccles)
Whinburgh	Winbrer
Wiveton	Wifton
Wood Dalling	Woodorlin' (along same lines as Pudnorton)
Worstead	Woosted
Wortwell	Wurtell
Wretham	Rettum (East and West)
Wymondham	Windum
Yarmouth	Yarmuff

There are many other potential pitfalls concerning places with similar-sounding names, as well as a batch of villages with the same name. Here are some useful tips on how to avoid confusion:

Bessingham is in North Norfolk – **Bressingham** is near Diss.

Booton is a small community near Reepham – **Boughton** is not far from Downham Market.

Bramerton is near Norwich – **Brampton** is three miles from Aylsham.

Brome is near Diss – **Broome** is near Bungay.

Dunston is on the A140 just outside Norwich – **Dunton** is three miles west of Fakenham.

Gillingham is near Beccles – **Gimingham** is a few miles from Cromer.

Griston, with its prison, is close to Watton – **Grimston** is seven miles east of King's Lynn.

Hanworth is five miles north of Aylsham – **Hunworth** is two miles from Holt.

Ketteringham is six miles south-west of Norwich – **Kettlestone** is near Fakenham.

Langham is six miles from Holt – **Longham** is five miles from East Dereham.

Roxham is near Downham Market – **Wroxham** is at the heart of the Broads.

Salhouse is near Norwich – **Salthouse** is on the North Norfolk coast.

Suton is a couple of miles from Wymondham – **Sutton** is near Stalham.

Thornage is a few miles from Holt – **Thornham** is between Hunstanton and Brancaster.

Don't muddle:
Bacton, Wacton and Waxham

Snetterton and Snettisham
Caston, Coston and Cawston
Flitcham and Litcham
Brinton, Briston and Brisley
Eaton and Easton
Tittleshall, Tivetshall and Titchwell
Ringland and Ringstead
Reedham and Reepham
Rougham, Roughton and Roudham
Thurne, Thurning, Thurlton, Thurton and Thurgarton
Hoe and Howe
Honing and Horning
Oxnead, Oxwick and Oxborough
Stoke Ferry, Stoke Holy Cross and Stokesby
Hingham and Ingham (and note that self-effacing Lessingham is next door to Ingham)

There are several 'twins' living some way from each other:
There is one Billingford near East Dereham and another one near Diss. You can find one Croxton three miles east of Fakenham and the other three miles north of Thetford. Look out for a pair of Hardwicks, one near King's Lynn and the other a few miles from Harleston. There's Roydon on the outskirts of Diss and Roydon a few miles from King's Lynn.

Don't confuse the Wittons, one near Norwich and the other close to North Walsham. There's also Witton Green, near Reepham and Witton Bridge at Happisburgh.

Norfolk has a couple of Hackfords, one with a Reepham flavour and the other close to Wymondham. Fritton near Yarmouth is a fair way from Fritton near Long Stratton.

Make sure you give the full name if you want to know the way to Oulton Broad near Lowestoft. You'll find Oulton on its own is a small community about three miles from Aylsham.

Newton's Law is useful. Newton Flotman is seven miles south of Norwich, Newton St Faith is four miles north of the city, there's Little Newton next door to Castle Acre and West Newton is on the Sandringham Estate.

If you fancy a testing contribution to a Norfolk quiz on village names, just ask your eager panellists for the names of the only two villages with as few as three letters. Put them out of their misery with Hoe, near East Dereham, and Oby, not far from Great Yarmouth. The latter is also known as Ashby with Oby and used to be incorporated with Thurne as well in the West Flegg Hundred. White's Norfolk Directory of 1845 says 'Ashby with Oby and Thurne, at the north-western angle of West Flegg Hundred, were consolidated in one parish in 1604, and now comprise 262 inhabitants, of whom 177 are in Thurne, 69 in Oby and 16 in Ashby'.

Norfolk boasts four Beestons – Beeston Regis, near Sheringham, Beeston St Andrew, near Norwich, Beeston St Lawrence, near Wroxham and Beeston-with-Bittering, seven miles from East Dereham.

Make sure you know which Burnham you are after. Lord Nelson, Norfolk's most famous son, was born at Burnham Thorpe. There are six more close to each other – Burnham Market, Burnham Norton, Burnham Overy, Burnham Deepdale, Burnham Ulph and Burnham Westgate. In fact, Burnham Overy is two villages, Overy Town and Overy Staithe... so you can have the choice of eight.

The Thorpe business is flourishing, with Thorpe St Andrew on the Norwich doorstep much the largest of the family. Thorpe Abbots and Thorpe Parva are both near Diss; Thorpe Market is a few miles from Cromer; Thorpe Row is near East Dereham; Thorpe-next-Haddiscoe is five miles east of Loddon; Thorpe End, on the fringe of Norwich, runs into Great Plumstead; Thorpe Marriott is the newcomer demanding attention on the other side of the city.

While several 'partners' live closely together – like North and South Creake, Little and Great Cressingham, East and West Bradenham - there are several exceptions to the rule.

East Bilney is near Dereham while West Bilney is close to King's Lynn. North Walsham is an expanding town in North Norfolk; South Walsham is a village in Broadland. East Dereham is the town at the heart of Norfolk; West Dereham is a small settlement near Downham Market. (Matters have not been helped there by the decision of the bigger Dereham, deemed rather arrogant in some quarters, to dispense with the 'East' from its name.)

There are other little twists. North Elmham is five miles from East Dereham (see how useful a full name can be!) while you have to go into Suffolk to find South Elmham. Little and Great Ellingham are neighbours near Attleborough – and there is an Ellingham going solo near Bungay.

Southwold goes its own genteel way on the Suffolk coast; Northwold is a long village a dozen miles from Thetford. Somerton and Winterton do rub shoulders not far from Yarmouth while it is a matter of regret to some that Norfolk does not yet boast as 'Springton' or 'Autumnton'.

Other points worth noting...don't confuse Barton Turf, near Wroxham, with Barton Bendish, between Swaffham and Downham. There's Belaugh near Wroxham and Bylaugh near East Dereham. Both small parishes and both pronounced 'Beloe' or 'Beeler'.

You will find East and West Runton between Cromer and Sheringham.

North and South Runcton and Runcton Holme are close to King's Lynn. East Ruston and Sco Ruston are a few miles from North Walsham. And don't mix any of those with East and West Rudham, a few miles from Fakenham.

Beware of the Swanton connection. Swanton Abbott, Swanton Morley and Swanton Novers are nowhere near each other. Old and New Buckenham are close neighbours near Attleborough. Then there's Buckenham Tofts near Thetford, and Buckenham on its own along the Norwich-Yarmouth railway line. It used to be known as Buckenham Ferry.

The Burgh family need careful inspection. Burgh on its own is near Aylsham, while Burgh Castle, Burgh St Margaret and Burgh St Peter are all close to Yarmouth. To add a bit more variety we have Burghapton, often spelled Bergh Apton, and they'll tell you it used to be billed as Burgh Apton in some old directories.

Don't muddle the Carleton clan – East Carleton, Carleton Forehoe, Carleton Rode and Carleton St Peter. (And there's a Carleton Colville not far from Lowestoft.)

Remember Cley is in North Norfolk while Cockley Cley is near Swaffham.

Eccles-on-Sea has an inland 'twin' near Attleborough.

Don't confuse Wood Dalling, Wood Norton, Field Dalling and Wood Rising. Then there's Woodbastwick, Woodton and the two Woottons near King's Lynn. Wolferton is where the trains used to stop for the Royal Family near Sandringham. Wolterton. with its splendid country house, is near Aylsham.

Little and Great Plumstead are a few miles east of Norwich. Plumstead on its own is between Holt and Aylsham.

Caister-on-Sea is next door to Yarmouth. Caistor St Edmund is close to Norwich. Note they are spelled differently.

Don't mistake Holme Hale near Swaffham for Holme-next-the-Sea.

Houghton-on-the-Hill is also near Swaffham, while Houghton St Giles and Houghton of Robert Walpole fame are Fakenham way.

Martham is in the Fleggs near Yarmouth. Marham, with its RAF associations is between Swaffham and Downham. Marsham, birthplace of Sir George Edwards, the farmworkers' leader, is near Aylsham.

The Meltons, Great and Little, are just beyond Norwich. Melton Constable, once at the hub of the local railway service, is six miles from Holt.

Saxlingham Nethergate is eight miles south of Norwich. Saxlingham is four miles from Holt.

Long Stratton and Stratton Strawless are well apart. So are Toft Monks, Toftrees and Toftwood.

Distinguish between Framingham Earl and Framingham Pigot, and Horsham St Faith and Newton St Faith. And always remember a Norfolk village may have a 'shadow' just over the border or further afield. For example, there is a Brampton close to Aylsham and another one not far from Beccles. Bacton on the Norfolk coast has a 'twin' near Stowmarket.

They may sound very similar, but Aldborough is near Cromer while Aldeburgh, with its wonderful music connections, is on the Suffolk coast.

SISTERS' DILEMMA

Three sisters, aged 91, 93 and 95 lived together in Norfolk. One night the 95-year-old ran herself a bath.

She put her foot in, paused and yelled: "Now, wuz I gettin' in the tub, or gettin' out?"

The 93-year-old called back: "Dunno, I'll come and see." She started up the stairs and then stopped. "Wuz I goin' up or comin' down?"

The 91-year-old sat at the kitchen table sipping tea and listening to her sisters. She shook her head and sighed: "I dew hope I never git that fergitful." She knocked on wood for good measure.

Then she yelled: "I'll come up an' help both o'yer sewn's I see who's at the door."

LESSON SEVEN
NORFOLK SHORTHAND

My early lessons in Norfolk shorthand were dished out with undisguised glee by elders of the village, including several relatives who spared little feeling when it came to summing up those falling short of proud family traditions.

"That'll larn yer!" or "Serve yew roight!" were the least you could expect in the wake of calamity involving some mundane practical task, like cleaning out a water tub and letting it roll over your left foot or taking a pail of swill to the pigs and being knocked over amid all the excitement.

It soon became clear that "rum dew" or "rum job" covered a multitude of unfortunate or unusual events, from a dramatic flare-up in the Middle East or sex scandal at Westminster to a tile disappearing from the cowshed roof or Billy insisting on buying a round twice in the same year.

Glorious understatement, a key component in the best Norfolk humour, coated pithy comments like "might he'bin wuss" when a lengthy list of disasters demanded attention in pub, shop, chapel, village hall or farmyard. It wasn't cruel indifference but more of a rural campaign to keep life in proper perspective, to leave whingeing and whining to that soft lot in town and city.

Wise old men of the fields didn't waste words on meteorological summaries. "Fresh" applied to a hurricane with snow flurries. "Damp" meant the monsoon season had come to stay. "Thongy" pointed to close or oppressive weather after three weeks of unbroken sunshine. Sugar beet workers would lift their heads at the end of marathon rows on muddy, frosty, flesh-shrivelling mornings and inquire politely of each other "Sweatin'?"

Country housewives also kept a tight rein on language and feelings when domestic duties ruled. "Thass how it is" sufficed as a verdict on global or parochial issues from hydrogen bombs to ration books if they felt little purpose would be served by further discussion. "So they say!", usually delivered with a knowing smile, carried so much implied criticism there was no real need to go on.

My favourite, still perplexing over half a century later, starred a couple of village women whose conversations invariably defied any rules of logical thinking. It was as if they were communicating in some kind of rustic code... "Are yew gorter cum ter bingo ternyte?" Short interval for deep thought. Then a deadpan "That orl depend..."

There it would end. No clues whatsoever as to what her decision might depend on. No follow-up inquiry from her friend looking forward to eyes down for a full house. I simply marked it off as a rum dew and anticipated the next revealing chat.

Of course, these shorthand examples come from an era when most Norfolk communities were bound together by common threads, sharing deep local roots and mannerisms and accepting their lot as largely inevitable. Exchanges reflected a brand of cheerful fatalism coupled with broad agreement that at least they lived in a relatively unspoilt corner of the kingdom, uncluttered by heavy industry or massive development.

Social and agricultural revolutions notwithstanding, there remains a fiercely protective streak in Norfolk, especially in rural parts, as natives suspect too many newcomers and visitors will destroy the very qualities attracting them in the first place. A powerful debating point not confined to God's Own Country but of extra relevance whenever the area is cited as ripe for a few thousand more executive dwellings.

Here's a crash course in current Norfolk shorthand to help foster a better sense of trust between native and newcomer. Allowances must always be made for the deceptively subtle style adopted by proud locals when confronted by what they regard as dramatic, and therefore largely unnecessary, change.

Comments most used by locals, most notably at parish council meetings, down the village pub, at the vicarage garden fete or in the bus shelter, are accompanied by helpful hints as to what they really mean:

"Hent sin yew round these parts afore..." It is abundantly clear that you are a complete outsider and we are at a loss to understand how you manage to get through passport control while the bridge was up. Did you bribe the guards? Don't let this homely smile fool you. I am a dedicated xenophobic. I would tell you as much if I could pronounce it.

"Thass fairly quiet about here..." We have always done things our way and woe betide the pushy beggars who try to change that! If you can't stand the sound of silence – along with crowing cockerels, spluttering tractors, excitable bullocks, church bells going like the clappers and Gloria's BSA Bantam – then it would be advisable to return to the rave-infested society you came from.

"We dew hev a few new houses..." This delightful village stands on the verge of being completely ruined by over-development with insensitive outside forces imposing their unnatural designs on an unsuspecting community with the acquiescence of district and county authorities and a government which wants everywhere to look just the same.

"We're still close to the soil..." Jack Piper is the last survivor of a proud agricultural tradition – and he only takes his old mare to help out with the harvest if the combine breaks down. Nearly everyone in the village used to work on the land. Now well over half of them don't have a clue where milk and eggs come from and can't tell the difference between wheat and barley. They all sing "All is Safely Gathered In", but very few even set foot in a stubble field.

"They're dun up Pightle Cottage..." Have you ever seen anything so pretentious in your life! They've got wheels that don't turn, lamps that don't light and plastic gnomes and concrete angels destined never to talk to each other. That orange patio doesn't look quite right and someone should tell these roadside vendors that "Tomatoe's and Cucumber's" should not be sprouting apostrophes.

"I'll hev a harf, thankyer kindly..." You would be extremely misguided in thinking we half-wits and peasants can be bought off so easily. Perhaps I ought to warn you that we have been known to sting strangers and newcomers for a short or two to keep the cold out. Especially in August. There will be no pity on tap should you have the audacity to try to curry favour again.

"Skool's still open..." You might have thought an educational establishment founded in 1870 and catering for over 60 pupils in a growing village would be safe. But parents, teachers, governors, pupils and the local newspaper have been forced to launch seven survival campaigns in the last decade. That's as well as raising funds for books, computers and slates for the roof. Next on the agenda – luxurious inside toilets.

"Parish cownsil's allus bizzy..." They were obliged to call out the police last month after that vote for more housing. It was alleged that some councillors bred and born in the village had gathered secretly at The Dewdrop Inn beforehand to plot tactics. Scuffles broke out when council chairman Grant "Bistro" Parmenter, a recent arrival from Braintree, surprisingly gave his casting vote in favour of more large houses.

"Wikker's a rum chap..." The Rev. Jasper "Otis" Reading, who we share with 12 other parishes, is from the evangelical wing of the Church of

England. He's organised harp lessons for the Golden Threads Club. They discuss herbal remedies and third world agriculture after choir practice. He gets them singing, swaying and clapping during Sunday morning collection so they don't notice how much they are putting on the plate.

"Football team's dewin' nicely..." The village side now have to be introduced to each other before kick-off because there are so many outsiders joining. Player-coach Monty Van Hyre flies over from Holland. Sponsors "Dialadwile Floor Cleaning Service While You Wait" promise to finance a new stand at the Cobweb Farm End if the lads win promotion and do well in the Genetically-Modified Crops Cup.

"We like new people ter muck in..." They move in. They know the lot. They take over. We tend to let them get on with it. And if they should lower themselves to ask for advice, we pretend not to know what they are talking about. It saves a lot of arguments.

"Reckun thass changin' a bit..." Last time I bumped into someone I knew in the village was at an Allotment Holders' Association sit-in at Holkham. I even forget who I am myself because nobody shouts out my name when I'm walking or biking down the street. We used to argue and fall out over nothing in the old days. That kept us going. You could make up over a half and get ready for the next bit of aggravation. Now you can go a whole month buying your own beer.

"A lot o' ole squit!" You make no more sense than any of the others who moved here in the hope of enlightening simple folk and pushing Norfolk into the twentieth century. We're not quite ready for that yet.

SMALL SCALE

Two Norfolk lads went on a fishing trip to Scotland. They rented a cottage, boat, rods and tackle.

After two weeks they'd caught just one small salmon.

"Horry, dew yew realise this pathetic little fish corst us about £500 apiece?"

"Oh, ah," Horry replied. "thass a bloomin' good job we only caught one onnem!"

LESSON EIGHT
TRAIL OF SURPRISES

Norfolk's enduring reputation as a pleasant place to live or explore brooks no serious opposition –even from those who mutter disparagingly about the Road to Nowhere being more like a rutted cart-track with tufts of grass down the middle.

Contrary to popular legend, natives rarely invoke the ultimate rule in self-preservation for all the goading and guying they have to endure, especially in summer.

"Clear orff back where yew cum from!" is but the last resort in any campaign to convince newcomers that a place can exude charm without mountains, motorways or metropolitan urges.

A growing number of home-grown characters, fully alive to the value of diversification in a county which gave the world Canaries and Linnets in football boots, have accepted gracefully and gratefully a dramatic surge in tourism since posh magazines decreed Norfolk could be more trendy than truculent.

I have watched numbers multiply along the blessed North Norfolk coast , caravans and Chelsea Tractors clogging up the centre of Cromer just long enough to spell out how quickly visitors can latch on to that old Norfolk habit of slowing down and smiling at complete strangers. Why, that might even lead to exciting cultural exchanges should someone show the slightest hint of impatience...

Heartening advances down the holiday trail must be celebrated, marking acceptance on either side that words like "grockle","peasant", "invasion", "missionary", "backwater", "inbred", "know-all", "dead-end" and "furriner" should come out of the locker only when absolutely necessary.

Mind you, it has been known for both parties to indulge in mild provocation simply to add spice to a pleasant day in the countryside or on the coast. It wouldn't be Norfolk without the odd straw-sucking rustic leaning on a gate to stop it falling over or an old salt holding court on the beach.

A dash of pretend ignorance or cheekiness on the part of the interloper with well-modulated tones and a map held upside down completes a memorable cameo of the eternal fixture between home and away.

Henry "Shrimp" Davies, lifeboat coxswain turned deckchair attendant and self-appointed area spokesman, loved to banter with holidaymakers

.winding them up but refusing to let them go until honour had been sat-isfied. He didn't mind crab boats travelling sideways or seaweed possess-ing powerful forecasting qualities if that amused his audience. Even so, he had the perfect answer for insults, cheeky or otherwise, bouncing his way as the North Sea growled or soothed in the background.

"Shrimp", nephew of legendary Cromer lifeboat coxswain Henry Blogg, excelled himself when a visitor, apparently trying to be whimsical, suggested Norfolk people did a splendid job in coming across as slightly less than worldly in dealing with folk from afar. The seaside stalwart par-aphrased that as meaning "proper sorft."

He countered swiftly with a jabbing finger, withering look and deliber-ately loud expostulation:" Sorft? We're sorft? Yew save up for 51 weeks o'the year, cum here for yar holiday and we tearke all that munny orff yew in seven days. An' yew still reckon thass us what are sorft?"

Travellers of a nervous disposition can avoid too much excitement or embarrassment by shunning fleshpots at hectic times. (Some were advised also to shun crabpots at all times when "Shrimp" was about). It remains a matter of deep mystery to countless hardened residents why so many pleasure-seekers insist on descending upon the same place at the same hour, particularly on Bank Holidays and at the peak of the sum-mer season.

Perhaps the rise of carnival fever has inflated perceptions by the briny but deadlock, however colourful or economically beneficial in the short term, can hardly be voted a reasonable price to pay.

Norfolk is a big county, able over the centuries to meet the shock of repeated invasions from Rome, Scandinavia, Germany, the Low Countries and Normandy, to recover from these onslaughts, absorb the invaders and turn them into proud Norfolk people. That should be warn-ing enough for modern holidaymakers and would-be residents willing to dig a bit deeper into a rich and rousing history.

With them in mind, and taking account of a burgeoning need to spread interest across a much wider area, I present an alternative tourist trail packed with surprises. Only those with an adventurous streak should wrap sandwiches, mark the map and accept yet again that dear old Norfolk loves to "dew diffrunt" These attractions are in no particular order of merit and do not follow any specific route . I have visited them all with family and friends over recent years, some many times to calm the soul after too much agitation on the popular highways:

Flint mines
It looks like a lunar landscape or wartime bombing range. But you have found one of the oldest industrial sites in Europe, an extensive group of

flint mines dating back to the late Neolithic period about four thousand years ago. Grimes Graves, near Weeting in deepest Breckland, seven miles north-west of Thetford, is dotted with grass-covered hollows. Beneath them are shafts from the bottom of which radiated galleries, where miners using antler picks extracted high quality flint. One of the mines is open to the public.

Although for safety reasons visitors are not allowed to crawl along the tunnels, it is possible to climb right down the shaft and see the seven galleries. Not for the upwardly mobile!

Pyramid in park

This has been dubbed the finest pyramid in England. It awaits those who can tear themselves away from the wonders of Blickling Hall, one of the county's top treasures near Aylsham. A stroll in the extensive park will bring an unforgettable reward. A stark, neo-classical pyramid mausoleum in the Great Wood contains the remains of John Hobart, 2nd Earl of Buckinghamshire, and his family. He made fashionable alterations to Blickling during his lifetime. He died under mysterious circumstances in 1793. The Blickling Hall guide book quotes Horace Walpole as saying that Lord Buckinghamshire "suffered from gout in his foot, dipped it in cold water and so killed himself."

The pyramid is over two miles from the car park –but well worth the exercise!

Cathedral of Fields

A magnificent monument to Victorian enthusiasm comes as a complete surprise at Booton, a small community on the outskirts of Reepham. The Cathedral of the Fields is the many-pinnacled parish church of St Michael the Archangel created by a gifted eccentric. Rector of Booton for 50 years, Whitwell Elwin began rebuilding the village church in the 1870s. His remarkable design included details from Venice and early churches in Egypt. He had no architectural training and no ability as a draughtsman- but the pinnacles and towers still draw gasps of admiration. It is cared for now by the Redundant Churches Fund although occasional services are still held. One of Norfolk's most extraordinary offerings described as "very naughty, but built in the right spirit" by leading architect Edwin Lutyens as it grew out of the fields.

Back on track

A bold Victorian adventure in the heart of the mid-Norfolk countryside is recalled by the name of County School on the outskirts of North Elmham. The school attracted pupils from all parts of the country and abroad and had its own railway station in 1884. Fortunes waned and the school closed in 1895. It caught the attention of London ship-owner E H Watts, a keen admirer of Dr Barnardo. Through his generosity the old school was reopened as Watts Naval Training School and that's how it stayed until 1953. Years of uncertainty followed before the school buildings were demolished.

County School has been revived with tracks re-laid and trains running. It is, in fact, located in the parish of Bintree but is well signposted on the road from Guist (remember how to pronounce that?) to North Elmham. Halfway up the drive, ascending towards the site of the school after leaving the level crossing and station, is a small cemetery. It holds headstones of boys who died within the vicinity of the school between 1904 and 1909. Aged between 11 and 14, it seems some were recaptured after trying to run away.

Visit this quiet corner –and be moved.

Solace in the city

An oasis of calm in the busy city, St Julian's Church with its attached cell was rebuilt after being almost totally destroyed by a German bomb in 1942. Down an alley between the bustle of Rouen Road and King Street in Norwich, Mother Julian's cell is a reconstruction of the room where she spent much of her life and, according to some historians, ministered through the window to the spiritual needs of visitors. The first recorded English authoress, her most noted work was the mystical Revelations of Divine Love.

She fell seriously ill in 1373 and was not expected to survive. When she did pull through she retired from the world into her anchorite cell and wrote of the revelations, or "showings" as she preferred to call them, received from God. She continued in prayer and contemplation until her death in 1415.

Dome teacher

Norfolk, of course, had a dome long before London got in on the millennium act. It sits now like an upturned dumpling on the edge of an old airfield not far from the coast. Along with the old control tower, converted into an office and stores, it's the only obvious survivor   of buildings which saw over two thousand service personnel stationed at Langham in 1945. The airfield was sold in 1961, mainly returning to agricultural use with turkey-rearing sheds built on part of the concrete areas.

The dome was used for anti-aircraft training. Appropriate film was projected on to the inside of the dome and trainee gunners practised dry firing at images on the film. Lighting and sound were available to make the exercise more realistic. To find this fascinating wartime relic, take the coast road east from Wells, turn right at Stiffkey and fork left towards Cockthorpe and Langham. The old airfield lies on the far side of Cockthorpe and the dome is close to the road.

While you are Langham way, visit the parish churchyard to see the grave of Captain Frederick Marryat (1792-1848). He spent his final years in Langham after a colourful naval career, writing seven novels including his classic Children of the New Forest.

Face in a case
A splendid collection of memorials to the Hare family demands attention in Stow Bardolph's Holy Trinity Church, just off the A10 Downham Market-King's Lynn road. To see the most startling of all go to the mahogany case that looks like a wardrobe in the north-west corner, open the half door – and meet the woman at the heart of a bizarre legend.

A face appears in the window. There's a grotesquely lifelike wax effigy of Sarah Hare clad in grubby bodice and scarlet hood peering out between tattered curtains. The story goes that she ignored conventions of the Sabbath back in 1744 and decided to do some sewing. She pricked her finger with a pin and died of blood poisoning at the age of 18. Before she passed away Sarah ordered that her memory should be kept alive by the life-size model...

In fact, she was about 50 when she died, so that statistic alone must throw serious doubts over the rest of the Stow Bardolph legend. But her haunting gaze defies you to take serious issue with it... or at least until you have left the family mausoleum.

A fatal duel
In a grove of trees at the side of the busy B1149 road, next door to a petrol station east of Cawston, you can hear echoes of a fatal feud between two leading local politicians. The Duel Stone, a short pillar surmounted by an urn, marks a clash on Cawston Heath in 1698 between Sir Henry Hobart of Blickling Hall and Oliver Le Neve of Great Witchingham Hall. Their quarrel built up over "words spoken in the heat of an election". Victorious Le Neve fled to Holland after wounding his opponent who died the day after the duel. Lady Hobart and supporters put a price of £500 on Le Neve's head. He later felt safe enough to return to England and stand trial. He was cleared of any blame.

Woodland shrine
A little chapel dedicated to the Virgin Mary is tucked away just inside a wood next door to gravel works in a mid-Norfolk hamlet. Czech airman

Paul Hodac, based in the county during the Second World War, built it as a gesture of thanks for deliverance from the Nazis. He bought Spread Oak Wood, an isolated and tranquil site at Bittering, and taught himself joinery and bricklaying. It took him seven years to build the chapel, mainly at weekends and during holidays. The shrine opened in 1983 and mass is held annually with folk of all denominations made welcome.

It takes some finding... follow the B1110 from East Dereham and fork left on the B1146 through Beetley .Turn left to Bittering. In the village, turn right, left and left again. Spread Oak Wood is on your left and is reached by turning left into the gravel works and backtracking along the trail to your right beside the wood's edge. The shrine is just inside.

Don't forget the way back after a spot of meditation and thanks for such a peaceful spot.

Tower of cubes

It looks as if a child has been busy with a box of bricks. A series of cubes piled one on top of the other in diminishing size make up one of the most unusual church towers in the country. Soaring above the desolate marshes at the end of a long track from Haddiscoe, it has been described variously as a folly, a monstrosity and a pyramid. One thing is certain –you cannot ignore it!

St Mary's Tower at Burgh St Peter serves as a memorial or mausoleum to Samuel Boycott, who built it in 1793 as a replacement for the earlier tower destroyed in a storm. He lies buried beneath it. The Boycotts were rectors at St Mary's from 1764 until 1899. There are brass memorials to the family in this church on the River Waveney, with Suffolk on the opposite bank.

That's close enough!

HE HAD TO ASK

The Norfolk vicar was showing a group of schoolchildren around the parish church.

They came to a big plaque on the wall, containing the names of men and women who had died during two world wars.

"What are them names?" asked Billy.

"They are the names of those who have died in the services," replied the vicar.

"Oh," exclaimed Billy, "Wuz that in th'mornin' or evenin'?"

LESSON NINE
CLOSER TO HOME

The rise of the pub quiz as a source of entertainment and social cohesion happily embraces a need to sharpen up on local knowledge. Norfolk compilers and competitive spirits lined up around the bar can play significant roles in making questions close to home essential ingredients of any worthwhile fraternisation programme.

I can report useful improvements since the end of the 1980s. A night of blank faces at Sheringham's Little Theatre told me how much parochial preaching had to be done. I was guest questionmaster for the popular town quiz final and the bonus was to be invited to set a round of my own choice. I posed six questions with a local flavour.

They all but drew a blank, in marked contrast to most of the other two dozen rounds as the finalists made short work of mathematics, geography, science and classical music. Mystified looks and eerie silences greeted my round. I didn't think questions about the birthplace of farmworkers' union leader George Edwards (Marsham) and the identity of the Norfolk humorist born at Potter Heigham in 1888 (Sidney Grapes) were all that testing.

I expressed my surprise and disappointment in an article penned for the *Eastern Daily Press*, also suggesting too little attention was paid in our schools to outstanding local characters. My sentiments provoked lively correspondence, one letter pointing out that as a journalist I had the time, inclination and opportunity to follow up obscure knowledge:"Like all people who have an interest in the subject, he thinks it should be common knowledge to all."

Well, I could not accept that being interested in people with Norfolk connections, many of them celebrated beyond the county boundaries, should be regarded as pursuing the obscure. I continue to feel strongly that their exploits should be recognised by many more people, especially those who live in Norfolk today.

It must also be reasonable to expect that those who claim to support composition of a local hymn of praise should learn a few of the verses or at least join in he chorus.

Enter the Singing Postman, that quintessentially Norfolk character who burst into the pop charts and the affection of the nation in 1965 with his catchy anthem Hev Yew Gotta Loight, Boy?

He still stars in pub conversations whenever the topics of authentic dialect, smoking, stage fright and sophisticated chat-up lines are in circulation. What might not be generally known is that Norfolk's Singing Postman was born in Lancashire in 1927 and died in Lincolnshire in 2000.

Turkey tycoon Bernard Matthews is another to make a colourful mark way beyond home soil. He bought a cheap incubator and 20 turkey eggs in 1950- and so hatched the beginnings of a food empire destined to transform the modern poultry industry and eating habits.

Bernard's main contribution to popular culture has been to make "bootiful" a household word and the subject of countless bad impressions. Norfolk dialect purists insist the label is gobbledegook and should read "bewtiful" or "bew'ful". A perfect debating point on a quiet night down The Dewdrop Inn.

Perhaps the most controversial personality always ready to prompt an argument is a Norfolk village parson who died over 70 years ago in bizarre circumstances. The diminutive Rev. Harold Davidson, who looked after coastal flocks at Stiffkey and Morston for over quarter of a century, was proud to be called The Prostitutes' Padre.

His speciality was saving fallen women. There were few in his part of Norfolk, so, for this purpose, he made regular trips to Paris and London. He often brought his catches back to Stiffkey and eventually stood accused of immoral practices. He became the nation's favourite source of scandal in the 1930s.

Davidson was tried before a church court at Westminster and ceremonially defrocked in Norwich Cathedral. Unabashed, he proclaimed his own martyrdom, first fasting in a cage as a sideshow in a Blackpool amusement park and then displaying himself in a barrel.

Finally, in a wonderful Old Testament climax, he preached at Skegness from within the cage of a lion which mauled him to death. He lies buried at Stiffkey where support for him among parishioners rarely wavered throughout the entire sensational saga.

Local history groups have mushroomed across the county in recent years, many of them strongly supported by newcomers determined to find out more about their adopted patch. Publications waving the parochial flag now demand plenty of shelves in local bookshops. There are no real excuses now for blank faces when Norfolk questions jostle for attention among all that pop and sporting trivia.

I find it wholly unreasonable that a resident of Swaffham should know the winner of the 1982 Eurovision Song Contest but remain ignorant of the fact that Howard Carter, who uncovered the treasures of the tomb of the Egyptian Tutankhamun in 1922, grew up in the town.

HOW TO SURVIVE IN NORFOLK

I consider it most impertinent that anyone living in my mid-Norfolk home village of Beeston might know the name of the current WBO light-welterweight champion but be unaware that Jem Mace, father of modern scientific boxing and a world champion, was born in the parish.

I deem it a pity that local youngsters who love football can reel off Manchester United's European honours but have no idea why Norwich City set the sporting world buzzing in 1958-59. They reached the FA Cup semi-finals as a Third Division club.

So, with those little moans to keep me going, I offer a crash course in vital Norfolk knowledge to brighten prospects at the pub quiz showdown, to act as a useful springboard for school projects and to encourage residents, old and new, to do the old place the honour of showing an interest beyond the best way to cook dumplings:

▶▶ The name "Norfolk" is of Anglo-Saxon origin and means the place of the North folk ("Suffolk" – place of the South folk).

▶▶ Norfolk stands fourth in size among the counties of England, covering well over 2000 square miles. The Norfolk coastline stretches for nearly 100 miles.

▶▶ There are more villages in Norfolk with a Saxon church than in any other county. Round towers are common and of nearly 180 in England, 119 are in Norfolk.

▶▶ Norfolk has over 24,000 recorded archaeological sites and 500 of them are protected by legislation. There are over 200 deserted villages in the county.

▶▶ There used to be 860 windmills and 100 wind pumps in Norfolk. About 50 are still standing more or less complete while many others are picturesque ruins. The old corn mill at Sutton, near Stalham, is thought to be the tallest surviving windmill in Britain with nine floors.

▶▶ North Elmham was the seat of a Saxon bishop from AD631 to 1071 before the bishopric moved first to Thetford and then, in 1096, to Norwich.

▶▶ Peddars Way is a long-distance path from Knettishall in Suffolk to Cromer on the north Norfolk coast. It follows the ancient Peddars way track through Breckland to the coast a Holme and has been extended from there along the coast to Cromer, a total of 65 miles.

▸▸ Weavers Way is a 15-mile route for walkers and cyclists between Blickling and Stalham, with extensions from Blickling to Cromer and from Stalham to Yarmouth through Broadland. The walk takes its name from the important weaving industry which used to flourish in the area.

▸▸ Poppyland is the name given to an area of the north Norfolk coast between Cromer and Sidestrand by journalist Clement Scott who "discovered" it towards the end of the nineteenth century. London's literary and artistic society made tracks for Poppyland after Scott's flowery articles in the *Daily Telegraph*.

▸▸ Wayland Wood, near Watton, is one of the areas of medieval woodland to survive in Norfolk. According to legend, it was the setting for the story of the Babes in the Wood.

▸▸ Breckland lies partly in Norfolk and partly in Suffolk, amounting to some 400 squares miles. Large flint-strewn open fields and derelict areas known locally as Brecks induced historian and naturalist William George Clarke to give the region the name of Breckland in 1894.

▸▸ The Broads make up Britain's largest and most famous inland waterway with over 125 miles of navigable rivers and broads. They resulted from extensive diggings for peat in the Middle Ages.

▸▸ The University of East Anglia was opened in Earlham, on the outskirts of Norwich, in 1963. Norwich City Hall was opened in 1938 by King George V1 and Norfolk County Hall was opened by Queen Elizabeth 11 in 1968.

▸▸ The Queen Mother opened the Royal Norfolk Regiment Museum in Norwich in 1990.

▸▸ There are seven places named Norwich and six Norfolks in the USA. You will find Norwich in Connecticut, Kansas, New York State (2), Vermont (2) and Long Island. There's also one in Ontario, Canada. You'll find Norfolk in Virginia (2), Maryland, Massachusetts, Nebraska and New York State.

▸▸ The Dutch engineer Cornelius Vermuyden built the first sluice at Denver, near Downham Market, in 1651 as part of a scheme to drain the fenlands owned by the Duke of Bedford. The oldest surviving sluice was built in 1843. Alongside is the Great Denver Sluice, opened in 1964.

▸▸ The first railway in Norfolk opened on 30 April, 1844, covering a 20-mile stretch from Norwich to Great Yarmouth. A train of 14 vehicles was assembled behind one of the little engines which took 50 minutes for the journey to the coast. It returned later that day to Norwich in 44 minutes –not far short of the present journey time.

▸▸ Britain's first modern beet sugar factory was built on the banks of the River Yare at Cantley, about 12 miles east of Norwich, opening for business on 11 November, 1912. It was largely due to the vision and determination of Dutchman Jerald van Rossum that the factory was built.

▸▸ The Norfolk police force was founded in 1839, one of the first professional bodies for rural areas in the country. As it grew the county constabulary absorbed the separate professional forces which once existed at Thetford, King's Lynn, Yarmouth and Norwich.

▸▸ Local television output began in 1959. BBC Television from All saints Green in Norwich first went out on 5 October. Anglia Television started broadcasting three weeks later. BBC Radio Norfolk was launched in September, 1980. Radio Broadland, the county's first commercial station, first went on the air in October, 1984.

▸▸ Ethel Colman became the first woman Lord Mayor of Norwich in 1923.In the same year, Dorothy Jewson became the first Norwich woman member of parliament.

▸▸ During the twentieth century three lay preachers from Swaffham Methodist Church became MPs –William Taylor, Sidney Dye and Albert (later Lord) Hilton.

▸▸ The first purpose-built cinema in East Anglia was The Gem at Yarmouth, completed in 1908. It later became the Windmill Theatre on the Golden Mile.

▸▸ Caister-on-Sea claims to have established the first real holiday camp in England. Fletcher Dodd opened his Socialist Camp in the coastal village in 1906, providing holidays for small groups from the East End of London. Dodd soon realised the potential of his idea. Wooden chalets replaced tents and dining and entertainment halls were built. In 1924 a week's holiday cost two guineas inclusive of all meals and transport from the railway station.

▸▸ The first Norfolk Agricultural Show was held in 1847 at Norwich Cricket Ground. The show was staged in a different town each year after 1862 but since 1954 all Norfolk Shows have been held on the permanent site at Costessey.

▸▸ At 160 feet, Cromer's parish church tower is the highest in Norfolk. St Nicholas at Yarmouth is the largest parish church in the country. It was badly damaged by fire bombs during the Second World War.

▸▸ Holkham National Nature Reserve is the largest in England, extending over 10,000 acres of marshes, dunes and intertidal mudflats along nine miles of coast from Burnham Overy to Blakeney

▸▸ Thetford Forest is the largest lowland forest in Britain, covering an area of 80 square miles and supplying about six per cent of timber harvested by the Forestry Commission. Planting began in 1922.

▸▸ The Burston School Strike was the longest in English history. Started by children at the village school near Diss in April, 1914, when their teachers Tom and Kitty Higdon were dismissed, it went on until just before the Second World War. The strike school is now a museum and meeting place.

▸▸ The highest point above mean sea level in Norfolk is Piggs' Graves crossroads at Swanton Novers at 331 feet. Roman Camp at Aylmerton, near Cromer, is next at 329.

▸▸ Carrow Road is Norwich City Football Club's third home. The club, formed on Tuesday, 17 June, 1902, played at Newmarket Road in their earliest days. They moved to The Nest for the start of the 1908-09 season. A disused chalkpit in Rosary Road was converted into a picturesque little stadium which was home until 1935.

▸▸   The Battle Area in Breckland, where troops still train, was created during the Second World War by the evacuation of five villages – Stanford, Lynford, Tottington, West Tofts and Buckenham Tofts.

▸▸   The Midland and Great Northern Joint Railway was known as the "Muddle and Get Nowhere" line. With a nostalgic sigh towards Melton Constable, once known as the Crewe of Norfolk, railway enthusiasts these days say it is "Missed and Greatly Needed".

▸▸   The terminal at Bacton on the north Norfolk coast was built in 1967 to receive natural gas from the North Sea.

▸▸   After eight years of intensive trapping, the Norfolk campaign to wipe out the coypu was declared an official success in January, 1989.The South American rodent was introduced into East Anglia for its pelt in 1929.

▸▸   Reepham has the unique distinction of having three parish churches in the same churchyard, although All Saints has been a ruin since a fire in 1513. The other two still there are St Mary's and St Michael's.

▸▸   Caister-on-Sea's lifeboat station was axed by the RNLI in 1969 but villagers, determined to keep their lifeboat history going, started an appeal to buy an independent boat, duly launched in 1972.

▸▸   Louis Marchesi founded the international Round Table movement in Norwich in 1927. By the time Round Table held their 40th anniversary luncheon, the movement had spread to 28 countries. It was the last public appearance for "Mark", as he became known, for he died in December, 1968.

▸▸   Thomas Bignold, who moved to Norwich from Kent in 1783, founded the Norwich Union a few years later. It became one of the largest insurance organisations in the world. The Bignold name continued to dominate Norwich Union until the retirement of Sir Robert Bignold in 1964.

▸▸   Nugent Monck founded the Maddermarket Theatre in Norwich in 1921. The former Roman Catholic chapel was transformed into an Elizabethan theatre.

▸▸   Luke Hansard, who went to London to become official print-er of all debates in the House of Commons, was born in Norwich in 1752.

▸▸   Dragon Hall in Norwich is the only medieval merchant's trad-ing hall known to survive in western Europe. It was built by Robert Toppes in the fifteenth century and is now maintained by Norfolk and Norwich Heritage Trust.

▸▸   Henry Blogg, Cromer lifeboat coxswain for 38 years, won more medals than any other lifeboatman. Three times he won the gold medal – the lifeboatman's VC – and four times the silver medal. Other awards included the George Cross and the British Empire Medal. During his years of service the Cromer boat went out 387 times and saved 873 lives. Blogg retired in 1947 after 53 years of service in all.

▸▸   William Cowper (1731-1800) is buried at East Dereham parish church. He wrote some of our most famous hymns and broke fresh poetic grounds despite frequent bouts of insanity. George Borrow, writer and champion of the gipsy way of life, was born at Dumpling Green in the town in 1803.

▸▸   Fakenham's nineteenth century gasworks have been restored for visitors. The town's museum of gas and local history provides the only surviving example in England of the small horizontal retort hand-fired gasworks. The works closed in 1965.

▸▸   From the earliest settlement, Yarmouth's street pattern has been based on a unique plan, a system of urban development not found in any other town in the country. For 900 years the old town,that part within the medieval wall, was laid out in ranks of buildings separated by three north-east streets and nearly 150 east-west "rows" – the famous Yarmouth Rows.

▸▸   The military first organised horseracing in Yarmouth on the South Denes in the eighteenth century. From 1810 regular meet-ings were held there until the present racecourse was built on the North Denes in 1922.

▸▸   Anna Sewell, whose only book, *Black Beauty*, became one of the world's best sellers, was born in Yarmouth in 1820. Her birthplace in the north-east corner of the market place, nestling in the shadow of the parish church, has been used as a restaurant and tea room in recent years.

▶▶ Gresham's School at Holt was founded as free grammar school in the 1550s and continued as such until1900 when it was transformed into the public school still flourishing today. Famous former pupils of more recent times include W.H. Auden and Benjamin Britten.

▶▶ Hunstanton has the unique distinction of being the only resort on the east coast to face west. It takes newcomers some time to get used to the apparent phenomenon of seeing the sun set over the sea instead of over land.

▶▶ In Hunstanton's Esplanade Gardens there is a memorial plaque bearing the names of 31 people who lost their lives in he 1953 east coast floods, 15 of them British and the other 16 citizens of the United States. An American named Reis Leming saved 27 lives and was awarded he George Medal.

▶▶ The Custom House, one of King's Lynn's most delightful buildings, was built in 1683 by local merchant Henry Bell. He was twice mayor of Lynn. It was originally used as an exchange and a statue of Charles 11 stands in a niche over the King Street entrance.

▶▶ Among famous people born in Lynn – writer Fanny Burney (born 1752); Margery Kempe, whose life is the first known autobi-ography in English literature (born 1373); explorer George Vancouver (born 1757); and John Mason, who founded the state of New Hampshire in USA (born 1586).

▶▶ Thomas Paine, the most outstanding political writer and rad-ical thinker of the late eighteenth century, was born in Thetford in 1737. For many years after his death he was disowned by his native town. Then in 1964 he was honoured with a gilded statue paid for by the Thomas Pane Foundation of America.

▶▶ Thetford was the fastest growing town in Britain in the 1970s. Overspill from London and new industries which accompanied the influx of population drastically altered the character of the town.

Thetford more than quadrupled its population between 1951 and 1981.

▸▸   The parish church of St Nicholas at Wells is a reconstruction. The old building was struck by lightning and largely destroyed in 1879. Among those buried in the churchyard is John Fryer, who served as Master of the *Bounty*, the ship at the heart of the most famous mutiny in maritime history. Fryer died in 1817.

HIRE PURCHASE

Gal Ethel had a sign outside her roadside cottage advertising ready-dressed chickens for sale. She sold them for the farmer up the lane.

One day while she was entertaining her friend Gladys, a stranger knocked on the door to buy a chicken.

"That'll be four pound" Ethel told him.

"Thanks" said the caller. "And I suppose you raised this bird yourself?"

"Yis, that I did anorl" declared Ethel.

"Oh, you bloomin' fibber!" said Gladys when her friend returned to the room. "Yew dunt raise them yarself."

"Well, I did that one," replied Ethel. "That wuz only three quid yisty!"

LESSON TEN
HISTORY LESSONS

I turn joyfully many times in these pages to squit as a source of solace in the wake of unpardonable changes to my beloved homeland.

Squit, that unique brand of cheerful nonsense honed on the need to face earnest questions, difficult times and dangerous impositions without tears or tantrums. It's part of a native make-up diligently applied to unnerve those who assume opposition must be loud and obvious.

Norfolk history is packed with subtle ploys to counter flagrantly hostile tactics or ridiculously popular misconceptions .Where else would locals smile benignly on hearing their county described as remarkable for little other than being "full of parsons and oak trees" or, as Horace Walpole put it so tastefully, occupied by "roast beef fashioned in human form"?

John Wesley, founder of Methodism, described Norfolk people as contentious and quarrelsome, especially in Norwich. Just because they didn't fill the collection plate when he preached at the Tabernacle in 1759, and left before all the chairs had been stacked neatly away.

Augustus Jessopp. writing in 1890 as Rector of Scarning, said;"Always shrewd, the Norfolk peasant is never tender; a wrong, real or imagined, rankles with him through a lifetime."

Exactly, Augustus. You know where you stand with a Norfolk peasant. Why explode violently and get it over all in one big go when a gentle simmer, a real grudge, can keep 'em guessing for as long as you like?

Noel Coward perpetuated the biggest calumny of more recent times when he penned the immoral line:"Very flat, Norfolk", thus giving those with nothing useful to say about the place the chance to say it on the back of someone very important in the communication business.

Meanwhile, Norfolk fresh-air enthusiasts continue to support brave mountain rescue teams, most notably in that hazardous range along the Acle Straight. High-minded actions speak louder than flat words.

One of the undoubted virtues of a grammar school education in Norfolk in the 1950s and early 1960s was scope for a young but passionate eccentric to flourish – as long as the joined-up writing was reasonably legible and essays were handed in on time. I took exceptional liberties with history, international, national and local, as soon as I realised lessons could be brightened with a bad pun and knowing smile. Enter Copernicus –"Dig that underwear! – and the Pedlar of Swaffham –"How fast did his bike go?" I questioned how it might be possible to have a civil war. I suggested history could be something that never happened written by someone who wasn't there. I marvelled at the thought of Sir Francis Drake circumcising the world with a 40-foot clipper.

Old habits die hard. My introductory course to Norfolk history, prepared mainly for serious-looking newcomers anxious to catch significant echoes from the past, has been described as "possibly misleading" by some venerable rivals on the lecture circuit. My response, stunningly simple in concept, is based on the premise that all thirsters after knowledge should be teased into exploring meaningful avenues of their own.

I put up the signposts. You find out if they lead anywhere. The perfect Norfolk compromise with a bit of fun to boot. Squit with purpose. History will judge if my elasticity has merit.

* * *

I start with warrior queen **Woadecia,** one of the first real people in Norfolk history. Extra rations of rouge, along with her charming little invention of a wheelie-bin with knives, did much to upset the invading Rum'uns. (They keep on coming.)

Woadecia has inspired legions of dyed-in-the-wool Norfolk patriots over the centuries and may well have been the driving force behind the initial Best-Crept Pillage Competition. Face-painting at village fetes certainly marks her colourful role in local history, while some still salute her sacking of London and subsequent setting fire to it by referring to the place as The Smoke.

The Paston Lettuce came to full fruition during the Wars of the Roses, which just goes to show how vegetables and flowers have mixed happily on Norfolk allotments since the fifteenth century. This outstanding winner should not be confused with the Runhall Bean, Holme Kale, Lady of Shallot or Norwich Onion (later to be used as the name for a large insurance company.)

Herbert de Lozenge is best remembered as the founder of Norwich Cathedral in 1096. He must also be credited with inventing a small but pungent cough sweet, experimenting with city congregations in order to keep interruptions to a minimum while he was preaching."Keep on taking the tablets, my friends" is believed to have been the text for his final cathedral sermon.

Sir Robert Whirlpool, our first Prime Minister, took 13 years to build Houghton Hall, the biggest country house in Norfolk completed in

1735.The project took so long mainly because Sir Robert hired famous French designer Jacques Coozie to install the latest bathtime luxuries in every room. Some claimed it was money down the plughole but important visitors from all over the world were tickled pink.

Turn-up Townshend married Sir Robert Whirlpool's sister and became a champion of progressive farming on retiring to his Norfolk country seat at Raynham. He inherited the estate and he title of Second Viscount in 1687.He earned his nickname through popularising a new kind of garb among his workers during the sugar beet harvest .By turning up the lower end of trouser legs, and so keeping them out of the mud, they were able to complete rows much quicker than those on neighbouring estates. Townshend also invented the four-course crop rotation to bring more variety to the menus in Burnham Market's fashionable coffee houses.

Thomas Pine was raised, suitably enough, in Thetford Forest before embarking on a dazzling career as political radical on the international stage. He never forgot his roots. His best-selling book Common Scents recalled the favourite Breckland flowers and shrubs of his youth while his Age of Raisin is considered the finest Norfolk recipe book of the eighteenth century. Rites of Man, a funeral guide for guillotine operators, did much to give the French Revolution an air of respectability.

Horatio Elsan, invariably celebrated as Norfolk's favourite son, did far more than earn a reputation as Britain's most honoured naval leader in history. He brought relief to thousands of ordinary seamen by inventing the transportable chemical toilet for use on the high seas. He first got the idea as a student at the Paston School in North Walsham while in detention for three weeks after failing a geography exam.

His affair in later life with society hostess Lady Christine Hamilton culminated in their appearing together in the very first television reality show "How Clean is Your Poop-deck?"

I could go on – but the proud book of Norfolk history is open for closer inspection among those who seek true enlightenment in an era when cheap celebrities and contrived events occupy far too many minds.

Find time to learn more of The Rick-burning Riots of Stratton Strawless (1831), Parson Woodforde's *Gluten-free Gourmet Guide* (1782), John Sell Cotman's New Painting by Numbers (1805) and Thomas Browne's *Easy Guide to the Norfolke Dialecte* (1656).

And don't ignore the county's time-honoured claim to be cherished as predominately agricultural after all that rape and silage.

LESSON ELEVEN
PRESSING MATTERS

Chester Bunson, born-again cynic and chief reporter of *The Bildmoor and Crammem Times*, was back from London. He had enjoyed a quiet weekend break away from the hurly-burly of Norfolk life. A flick through the office diary told him it could be another hectic spell in the endless search for the area's top news stories.

Just mild disappointment, then, as the morning rounds provided only moderate pickings. A district planning committee discussion on six more new village developments of around a thousand houses apiece went down the same old track. All in favour – except Diehard Grimshaw.

He took his role far too seriously as "custodian of the local cause". How often did Chester wish he had never anointed him thus in his Insider column three years before!

Objections on ethnical as well as ethical grounds took the debate into higher realms of abuse than usual, with a purple-faced Diehard alleging that certain elected representatives and all council officers were in the pockets of the developers.

"An' if that ent a cawse fer shearme an' whoolsearl resignearshun, then I dunno what is. We myte jist as well cleer orff hoom or down the pub an' let the demerkratic prosess forl ter bits."

The committee chairman reminded Mr Grimshaw that uttering Chaucerian oaths would hardly aid his cause, and he ought to be proud so many people wanted to move to Norfolk to share the beauties none of them could ever take for granted.

Couple of paragraphs here, mused Chester, and a little bit for the column along Realists v Idealists lines. He headed for a hearty lunch at The Rampant Ferret, the refurbished hostelry where the editor, the irascible Mr Ruby, was chatting to Rotary colleagues in a rapidly-filling bar.

Mr Ruby held court with all the aplomb of a seasoned politician on the hustings as questions poured in about the latest edition of his paper.

In fact, he made it more of a performance than it deserved, for most of the inquiries or comments were little more than amiable asides designed to impress an important and influential figure. The real challenge was to say something witty enough to find its way into next week's leader column.

The editor, tiring of a succession of flat contributions, conjured

Chester's first half of bitter on to the counter within seconds. Not a word. Not a glance. They had fashioned a kind of pub telepathy over the years, and it seemed to transfer itself to whoever was behind the bar. And Mr Ruby knew a full pint would be waiting and frothing next time he stretched out a hand.

"Good weekend, Chester?" More of a statement than a gentle probe, so the chief reporter carried on tucking into his Beef Stroganoff.

"Could be a nice little yarn blowing up at Mildew Patch – you know, across the playing field and down that lane where the old brush factory used to be? That old biddy, Granny Trundle, she's refusing to leave..."

Chester opened the file in his head. Granny Trundle – herbal remedies – ancient local family – unsubstantiated reports of witchcraft – husband died about 300 years ago – she refused a chance to appear on a wireless documentary about colourful country characters.

"Compulsory purchase order sorted out months back, so she can't say there hasn't been time. Always be victims of progress, I suppose, but we've been waiting since the war for that ring road."

As the voice tailed off, Chester made a mental note under "possible human interest, with pic.", drained the last of the beer and strode to the police station.

The call yielded a spate of minor skirmishes over the weekend, including 34 arrests at the local football derby between Bildmoor Rovers and Crammem United. As this figure alone represented well over twice the average attendance at Mischief Meadow, Chester assumed it must be a mistake. In any case, the charity cup match would be replayed next Saturday, and he'd send young Simpson to keep an eye on proceedings.

Chester returned to the newspaper office to check the second post and to sort out the first editorial chore of the week, the gardening notes by Digger. As usual, they looked as if they had been written with the wrong end of a pitchfork. He chastised the drinks machine for still issuing short measure on the hot chocolate side.

Just occasionally, when it was quiet in the office and on the street outside, Chester would allow himself a little swig of nostalgia, early 1950s vintage.

On his old trade bike to collect the news items. Cups of tea and shortcakes galore and a drop of homemade parsnip wine while they waited for the photographer on diamond wedding duty.

Young Simpson would have to cut his teeth on such things. But it wasn't the same, even if Diehard Grimshaw kept telling the young'uns it either was or ought to be. Prosperity had followed all the rural promise he'd reported over the decades, but there were still pockets of resistance, still lingering fears of anything new or different...

The telephone burst in on his reflections. It was Pilgrim Parker, retired car park attendant, secretary of two bowls clubs and main raffle organiser at The Rampant Ferret.

"Hello, Ches – thought I'd better give you a tinkle just in case there's anything in it. Bit of a commotion at Mildew Patch. That barmy old beggar, Granny Trundle, she's gone and barricaded herself in, they say. Cop car and ambulance heading that way. Thought I saw Perkins of The Bugle hanging about."

Those final words catapulted Chester out of the office. He ran all the way without once considering the possible consequences, and also broke his own golden rule by not leaving a note to tell his colleagues where he'd gone.

Perkins, self-styled ace reporter on the Newhamlet Bugle, the paper working hard to make inroads into the Times' patch, stood teasing with an open notebook. The police sergeant and ambulanceman tried hard to look relaxed, but constant thrumming on the bonnets of their respective vehicles betrayed growing anxiety.

"She refuses to see anyone but you." Chester peered round to see where the remark was going. "Hold the front page, Chester! The old girl wants to offer you a world exclusive. Reckon she's forgiven you for not being sired or born in Norfolk, my ole bewty!"

Perkins scowled as the chief reporter of the Bildmoor and Crammem Times crunched up the path to the front door of the pretty little claylump cottage. An upstairs curtain twitched.

Chester Bunson felt the sort of tingle he hadn't experienced for many years, a mixture of excitement and apprehension. He turned to catch a glimpse of a lorryload of workers disembarking beyond the straggling privet hedge. Did Granny Trundle have the powers to make them disappear?

He could hear her shuffling to the door.

GOOD OFFER

The village school register was full. The classroom was packed. The teacher said to a lad who came to see her: "It's very generous of you, young Charlie, but I don't think your resignation would be much help in this situation."

LESSON TWELVE
THE BEER FACTS

We were sipping the last of the summer lager.

"I am not a lout" announced Compost, sleeving away the froth in a manner that suggested he was unlikely to be asked to join the Booker Prize judges next year.

"I drink to be sociable, not to nurture the spirit of rebellion in the darker corners of my being. I am not a blotto on the Norfolk landscape."

He was stung into verbosity by my inference that the older generation ought to set a better example to the ever-growing legion of thirsty youngsters.

"You forget the essential difference" he snapped. "They won't listen to their elders .We didn't get a choice –just a thump round the lug if we dared to argue."

Had that proved a miracle cure? Did seeing stars make him see the light? Was brain damage preferable to the odd hangover or cirrhosis of the liver?

"Perhaps it's daft to compare two extremes, the downtrodden youth of my day and the demolition yobs of the present era... but if I'm pushed, really pushed, and you invest in a half of my choice, I'll tell you why we got a marginally better deal."

Compost was serious. He stroked his left ear as if that was the key to open the Aladdin's Cave of his past. He looked straight at me. But he was years away.

"In the first place, the beer was better when I started serious drinking, and you learnt very quickly to respect the brew. To know your limits. Straight from the wood... wholesome, round taste, consistent... and the whole pub atmosphere went with it.

"None of this guzzling out of cans and bottles along the street, shouting and swearing and chucking the empties over the nearest garden wall. We loved our outdoor drinking in the proper place at the proper time-in the harvest field. And I don't recall anyone throwing a pewter pot at a rabbit snouting round he shoofs."

I was reluctant to daub my brush cross such a delightful pastoral canvas. But it was necessary to keep a balance.

"Come on, people got drunk in those days and pub trouble often spilled over outside. And you can't ignore the way drink made its marks on the domestic front. Breadwinners coming home short of money but full of beer and nastiness..."

Compost swallowed hard and released his fist from the freshly-filled mug.

"Yes, some homes had to put up with a lot of that, and that's why the Temperance movement and the Methodists preached strongly against the evils of the demon drink and tried to get us to sign the pledge.

"But some people will abuse it, whatever the age, whatever the conditions. Just remember, boy, times were much harder then. We had to make our money last. Couldn't snap our fingers and wait for a handout"

He jingled his change, peered round the bar and let his mood alter.

"Look at this lot-all earrings and personal stereos and microwave hairstyles. They don't talk to each other like we used to. They don't drink for company like we had to."

I guessed what was coming next, recalling Compost's contempt for most aspects of the age of mobility. He had confessed to a burning desire to set up an alternative body to East Anglian Roads to Prosperity, calling it Leave Us on the Single Track to Nowhere.

"They don't grow into a pub these days. Flavour of the month for a couple of nights, and then they're off to the next trendy watering hole. Blarst, we took over from our fathers and uncles and big brothers, and they'd moved into them seats left empty by their fathers and uncles and big brothers"

I was ready to mime the bit about war and pestilence and the old ways.

"Only war and pestilence kept us away. Now, you don't know a quarter on'em drifting in and out. How on earth can you keep the old ways alive if there's no-one to pass them on to?"

Compost was hurt, as if he had just discovered the reason for the end of an era. It was my job to cheer him up, to refresh the parts he could no longer reach for himself.

"People have more choice these days and they like to go round to see what's on offer. But only the good pubs will survive, combining the best of the old and the new. Pubs with a generation gap, especially in the country, will go to the wall"

I didn't know how much of that I meant but he seemed encouraged enough to threaten a movement towards the bar in the name of a refilling operation.

Then the jarring tones of the latest inter-galactic feud on the machine up the corner brought him back to his senses. I offered to buy.

"I'll just have another mouthful" he said."You'll have to make do with a pint" I suggested. One more round of meaningful banter. I let rip.

"Are you trying to tell me there were no little irritations in your young days? Nobody dropping in to take the edge off a happy little session and force the landlord to consider early retirement? Did every game of dominoes or phat inspire impeccable sporting behaviour?" I kept going.

"Can't you try to recall one night of raw emotion, at the end of harvest for instance, when familiarity bred a little contempt? Can't you remember one wet dinnertime when beer was in and sense was out? Didn't you ever fall over that old threshold and wonder if you were coming or going?"

Compost grunted. Obviously as close to appreciation as I was likely to get, or as near to a confession without placing him in the old village stocks and threatening to put a by-pass through his allotment.

The good old drinking times, long before 24-hour opening, bar meals and big brewery takeovers, must have been punctuated with little disagreements

Compost and his contemporaries are quick to denounce the lager louts without finding the heart to recall the rum rogues, stout troublemakers and victims of mild mayhem staggering across the pub scene of yesteryear.

Perhaps it was more confined to specific areas and therefore easier to control. Perhaps there was more comradeship in smaller and tighter-knit communities to help take the sting out of difficult situations .Perhaps there were more people anxious to preach self-respect and tolerance.

Perhaps they faced exactly the same problems but made less of them. In any event, they had one priceless extra asset, sadly neglected in today's high-speed world.

The pony-and-trap personal delivery service could function with or without specific instructions. Even Compost will own up to a few rides home he can't remember.

Only on one occasion did the pony make any fuss-when Compost spent an entire September night asleep in the trap. Yes, the old pony did come to the end of its tether.

But, as far as we know, that was the last of the summer whine.

LESSON THIRTEEN
CUSSED CORPS

One of the harshest indictments of newcomers' behaviour on being afforded a hearty welcome to the finest county of them all came, surprisingly, shortly after the Second World War.

H.J.Harcourt, writing in the fledgling *Norfolk Magazine* in 1948 – it started life as The Norfolker, but readers voted that a clumsy title –summed it up thus: "Strangers who come into our midst are inclined to treat us with benevolent condescension or with undisguised supercil-iousness –and then expect us to acclaim them as saviours and the harbin-gers of civilisation."

Some will affirm useful lessons have been learnt since, although Norfolk still has to put up with plenty of ribbing about being on the road to nowhere and working hard to keep the old drawbridge intact. I sus-pect some of these "backwater" comments are born out of envy.

Even those in the vanguard of the Development Express roaring through parts of the county in recent decades must have caught at least a fleeting glimpse of what is being replaced.

There's also now an element of admiration in backhanders like:"The only way to lead Norfolk people is first to find out which way they are going –and then march in front of them." It's one thing to be noticed for being different-and to be amusingly chastised for it –but Norfolk stal-warts draw the line at being asked to apologise for following natural instincts.

I recall one frustrated newcomer soaked in missionary zeal saying to a parish meeting packed with immovable natives:"You have a real problem –you have no talent for surrender." At once, a pat on the back and a kick in the shins. A double-edged remark that might have been specially mint-ed with Norfolk's cussed corps in mind.

Admired in one breath and attacked in the next, they continue to square up to tactics which might weaken or even break lesser mortals. There used to be two opening gambits in dealing with the Norfolk agi-tator always moaning about the rape and pillage of his domain by prop-erty barons, pushy incomers and various other insensitive creatures.

A contemptuous sniff or a patronising tap on the head was normally enough to send him shuffling towards some dark corner to mouth ancient oaths and to contemplate the diminishing role of a rural sage.

Buy him a half, put it down as "planning gain" on the progress ledger, agree it is a hard old world nowadays... but that's the way the dickey crumbles. Buy him another half, tell him to get his name down for the proposed Hemlock Pastures sheltered housing and say it hurts you far more than it hurts him.

Now it takes sharper ploys to put down an uprising. Traditional protesting methods are being coated in subtlety. For instance, many who used to think you had to get hoarse and turn six shades of purple to make a point now know the value of a nudge, a wink, a smile or a well-directed whisper.

That should not be construed as a form of capitulation. On the contrary, this marked change in approach can confuse the opposition to such a degree it leads to strange little spells of relatively peaceful co-existence.

The cynic might suggest the exploited are becoming as crafty as the would-be exploiters. The optimist will claim the urge for showdown is being overtaken by the spirit of compromise. Not all developers are pin-striped, hard-hearted speculators and spoilers. Not all natives are straw-sucking, buskin-clad peasants who can recall antics of the English Land Restoration League towards the end of the nineteenth century

The indigenous old guard have been joined in some areas by battalions of newcomers ready to help preserve what they moved for in the first place. Indeed, a clutch of local watchdog groups have blossomed as a direct result of this new alliance.

Extra numbers mean more influence, and this one area where the region's dramatic growth could yet prove a strange kind of blessing. When enough cry "Enough!" the message may seep through from Weeting and Wymondham to Whitehall and Westminster.

There have been sufficient claims about the "greening" in all thinking in all political parties to nurture healthy scepticism on all fronts. But if there are lasting benefits to come we should salute those with the nerve and foresight to shake the ecological ladder from the bottom.

Attitudes have changed. There's now far more likelihood of a vigorous debate over any development plans than a few years back when it was all too fashionable to shrug shoulders and claim it simply wasn't worth objecting.

Norfolk communities large and small are discovering a collective conscience to counter juicy offers from those who persist in thinking you can do what you like eventually if your crock of gold is large enough. (Certain supermarket giants push their luck and cash unashamedly.)

The more acceptable face of development smiles on areas where it replenishes and improves, where it finds harmony with the spirit as well as the look of the place. Perhaps that welcome dose of sense and sensitivity was inspired by Prince Charles, who does not shun the special requirements of rural parts in his regular tirades against glib uniformity.

He visits Norfolk often enough to appreciate how uncluttered charm keeps on colliding with complex challenges unleashed by the kings of market forces.

One powerful theory goes that people are bound to be drawn to pleasant parts, to live, to work, to retire, to visit, and these freedoms should be positively encouraged at a time of considerable population movement.

But what of the freedom of those descended upon from a great height to demand enough leeway to retain some degree of local pride and identity? Why should they be dismissed as eccentric left-overs .tired old grumblers, when so much obvious damage can still be caused?

They care passionately about where Norfolk is going as well as where it has been. They are entitled to draw attention to some of the follies of the past in the reasonable hope of avoiding too many additions or repetitions.

Room for compromise and co-operation, yes, but there can be no connivance, no coercion as far as Norfolk's cussed corps is concerned.

They have no talent for surrender, a glorious fault worth preserving, and a problem worth advertising while the forces of change continue to hurt much more than they enhance.

TOUCHING SCENE

An old Norfolk poacher fell seriously ill. His arch-enemy, the gamekeeper, decided to pay a visit.

Almost at his last gasp, the poacher consented to be reconciled with the gamekeeper. A touching scene followed in which both men shook hands warmly in mutual forgiveness. The gamekeeper was called back as he reached the door.

The old poacher, raising himself in bed gasped: "Jest yew remember, Walter, if I should happen ter git better - orl this is orff!"

LESSON FOURTEEN
SERIOUSLY STYLISH

Norfolk, so often the butt of metropolitan witticisms about flat vowels, bad roads, noisy turkeys, red-faced farmers, truculent tractors and inbreeding, is stirring to the thrilling possibility of becoming seriously stylish.

At least four households just outside the Burnhams have cancelled *The Land Worker* and *Methodist Recorder* from their newsagents and asked for introductory offers to *The Field*, *Vogue*, *Tattler* and *Westminster Gazette*.

Fifteen former wherrymen from the Dilham area have pooled their redundancy monies to invest in a yacht marina, restaurant and floating nightclub venture in Old Hunstanton,

A dozen ex-trappers have formed a consortium to arrange coypu-hunting safaris across grazing land at Brisley. A lottery grant and big-game licence are awaited.

This is but the start of a "Nouveau Norfolk" campaign destined to blow away the cobwebs of suspicion and dust of insularity besetting the scene since surprise visits by vicious Vikings and dastardly Danes.

This fresh spirit of ambition, styled largely out of economic necessity in parts of the county where decimal currency has yet to be fully accepted –Winfarthing and Quidenham lead the resistance –is a key plank in the building of Norfolk's reputation as a truly appealing quarter.

Of course, it is a dual-carriageway to this Promised Land, and those who would be correctly addressed after fleeing from the capital and its sprawling tentacles must travel in the same direction and at roughly the same speed as their provincial partners.

This means an end to traditional warring over street lighting, sparring over nominations for the parish council and tarring all natives with the same brush.

Weekenders and second-homers, so often the targets of misguided abuse when property prices soar and bingo sessions are cancelled because of dwindling support, must make themselves available for carol singing, clearing away tables after bridge tournaments in the village hall, running "drench the wench" at the church fete and organise petitions against too much development and closure of the local delicatessen.

This sort of give-and-take can only enhance Norfolk's right to be taken seriously as a member of the smart set. Too much take from either side will throw a shadow over the plumpest partridges and any new wallpaper range inspired by Bacton gas terminal or Yarmouth's Golden Mile.

There are also exciting hopes for the county to break into sport's premier division following Skeyton's surprise bid to host the Winter Olympics in 2016. The fine parish of Trunch is being urged to go for the 2222 World Cup football finals, not least because there would be no problems in persuading their immediate North Norfolk neighbours to build stadia for the earlier rounds. Gimingham, Trimingham, Knapton, Northrepps and Southrepps are others in that famous bunch .FIFA could soon learn the old rhyme.

Beetley expects to be added to the list of Test Match cricket arenas. A better track record than Old Trafford for weather, but the nearby rural life museum at Gressenhall offers an attractive alternative if it should rain.

British Grand Prix action could well be shared between Barton Bendish, Kilverstone and Carbrooke. Open Golf at Etling Green, near Dereham, or Three Holes, near Upwell, is a distinct possibility.

There's also animated talk of world canoeing championships at North Creake (without a paddle), the Boat Race switched to Dilham canal, tag wrestling at Flordon, Grand National at Horsey, athletics at Runham, with drug-testing at Pott Row, and angling championships at Wormegay, picking up rod and reels at Tacolneston.

If these sporting spectaculars take off – and fringe benefits could include international television coverage and new rural bus routes – other locations will be keen to get on the "honey pot" map, playing host to a conference, seminar, show or exhibition best suited to its name.

Crufts would be ideal for Clippesby. The British Medical Association couldn't fail to enjoy Feltwell. Bell ringers would descend on Pulham St Mary. The Do-It-Yourself Society could take the stage at Shelfanger. Funeral directors to Paston. The Magic Circle to Howe. The Police Federation keeping a summer date at Melton Constable. The Divorced and Separated finding a shoulder to cry on at Ditchingham.

Yes, these are tingling times for the movement designed to transform dear old Norfolk from a sleepy backwater into the place where everyone wants to be seen. How priorities change. We used to be proud of holding down fourth place in this little league table:

The North for largeness.
The West for wealth.
The South for buildings.
...But the East for health!

LESSON FIFTEEN
THE TROSHER PRIZE

Norfolk's glowing reputation as a haven for creative spirits makes plenty of allowances for serious literary figures well versed in dealing with the picaresque, stream of consciousness and social realism.

Even so, there's ample room to follow the torch lit by Disraeli, never backward in coming forward, when he told the Trosher Prize judges:"When I want to read a good book, I write one." That heralded a new era in self-aggrandisement.

The Trosher Prize? Rather overshadowed these days by the likes of the Booker and the Whitbread, but still highly regarded as the first to prick balloons of literary pomposity and feature volumes truly meant for the common reader. Happily, the competition continues, albeit in modest form these book-laden days.

Herbert Nathaniel Trosher, Norfolk landowner and national benefactor, made but two stipulations when he launched his revolutionary idea of offering "ten good sovereigns for ten good chapters" in 1829. He had to understand the work in its entirety and at least 20 pages of "clean script in legible joined-up writing" had to make reference to some aspect of Norfolk life.

Trosher Prize judgement parties, as they soon became to be known, invariably lasted three or four days and nights. All participants were invited to read extracts from their manuscripts and then faced probing questions from Herbert and his book-loving cohorts.

It didn't matter if the work had not been published, for as Norfolk's literary guru always emphasised with a twirl of that famous ginger moustache, sorting out the wheat from the chaff was as much a duty in the drawing room as it was on the threshing floor.

Perhaps the most celebrated Trosher Prize victor was Charles Dickens, who met all the requirements and discovered a deep affection for public reading when he treated the judges and a packed gallery to choice pickings from *David Copperfield* in Yarmouth's Royal Hotel.

Undoubtedly the most notorious "failure" was Victor Hugo, who presented himself in 1856 as an East Dereham exile who had penned *Les Miserables* as a tribute to William Cowper's efforts to cope with fits of despair the previous century. He was given top marks for invention – but disqualified for impersonation.

George Borrow, Anthony Trollope, Henry Rider Haggard, Arthur Ransome, Wilkie Collins, Anna Sewell, John Betjeman and Arnold Wesker were among other popular writers to catch the judges' eyes over the years.

Dorothy L Sayers' failure to impress remains a major mystery while Virginia Woolf's nomination in 1907 continues to provoke intense argument among devotees of the Bloomsbury Group. There are those who claim Clement Scott's appearance on the shortlist a decade earlier for his "Poppyland" offerings did far more than any tourist trade literature to popularise that area around Cromer.

Over a century later, North Norfolk again took prime position on the Trosher Prize podium when Sid Kipper's epic *Crab Wars*, an eagerly-awaited follow-up to *Prewd and Prejudice*, related what happened when the towns of Cromer and Sheringham fell out.

"Buckles were swashed, bodices were ripped and derring-do was done... and it was personal for Cromeo and Sheriet, two young lovers thoroughly parted by the hatred" Other memorable characters included Blake Vincent, thrust into the job of Town Crier just as his voice was breaking, and The Market Forces, a gang of persuasive young men who demanded much and supplied little.

No wonder one of the judges suggested :"Sid Kipper has an outer malice that conceals an inner beauty and warmth" The author, in the section marked "Forewarned", claims it has everything needed in a good story .." just enough sex and violence to keep the vicar happy, but not enough to worry my old mother. It's got lots of love interest and lots of hate interest too, which is just as much fun."

Traditional Trosher Prize virtues all contestants would do well to observe in a competition approaching its 180th chapter. There are only three finalists in the race for fame and fortune this year, but I am convinced old Herbert would be delighted to note all three contenders are unpublished, unsung, unassuming youngsters from an evening creative writing course somewhere near Thetford.

There was one other entry from a poultry farmer called "Pullet Surprise", but it was felt this could cause confusion with another well-established contest.

I have read all three entries but as one of the judges it would be invidious for me to express a preference or indicate where the votes might go:

Acid Drop Party, by Bonnie Ladd, tells how a group of pensioners in sheltered housing organise secret sessions of sin in the recreation room after midnight. Efforts to involve a reluctant warden in their nocturnal adventures provide the main thrust of the plot and chief comic elements.

Defiance of a regimented world spreads way beyond the distempered walls of Antimacassar Pastures. A surprise final act, lit by a spectacular storm along the Norfolk coast, may carry too much dark humour for some tastes. It says more for social attitudes than social services, although regular debates over the role of old folks' homes can't do sales any harm.

From Rush-Hour With Love, by Juan Wayye, is a bitter-sweet episode set against the backcloth of a Norfolk city's congestion problems. Donald, an accountant, and Nina, a photographic model, are brought together for a few minutes each day by the commuter crawl. It traps them – but gives their fantasies freedom.

They communicate only with glances, smiles and tentative little waves, but they start building respective new worlds out of these fleeting exchanges. One fine morning, a park-and-ride scheme is introduced. They are forced to talk at length to each other. A twist in the tailback.

Wish You Were Herr, by Gregory Upton-Fishley, is a fast-moving satire on much-vaunted plans to use tourism as a panacea for all economic ills in a rural area. When an important German visitor disappears after the opening of a new leisure village, local opponents of the development are accused of orchestrating the whole business.

Indeed, the German has been kidnapped 50 years to the day after the outbreak of the war and is being held in a nearby redundant church. His captors, a bunch of para-military hoodlums, do everything possible to keep suspicions focused on the locals.

Proof, methinks, there's plenty of good Norfolk reading well away from the Booker highbrow circus. And a perfect incentive for creative newcomers to Norfolk to put pen to paper with power and purpose.

HELP YOURSELF

At a Norfolk church hall gathering a vicar stacked up a pile of apples on a table with a sign saying: "Take only one apple, please – God is watching."

At the other end of the hall there was a table full of sausage rolls and shortcakes. Little Horry placed a sign by it saying:" Take all you want – God is watching the fruit."

LESSON SIXTEEN
SLEUTH... MISS MARDLE!

Miss Mardle tugged back the net curtains. A commotion near the duckpond was no more than an excited terrier chastising feathered foes for refusing to play properly on dry ground. With that little mystery solved, she smiled at the prospect of a light breakfast and gentle rustle of the newspaper before work started in earnest.

The call that brought her to Mayhem Parva in one of the Norfolk's more rural corners lacked nothing in confidence. "You will help us – or we'll tell the North Runcton Crime Writers' Circle you are a complete fraud!"

She had chuckled at their cheek, hired a sit-up-and-beg bicycle for a week, packed a rustic phrasebook in the saddle bag and pedalled into the unknown. A slight figure determined to crack one of the biggest mysteries of her glittering career.

The Case of the Disappearing Norfolk Character.

Ephraim Edwards gave an exaggerated smack of the lips and banged his tankard on the bar of the Four Ferrets.

"I'll get that. Usual poison?" Clive the computer commuter in generous mood. All pullover and pipe and an expert on the thatched space invaders, he grilled Ephraim every night for juicy local titbits.

Ephraim invented little stories every night in the face of such relentless curiosity.

"We'll get that. Usual poison?" The regular ritual was in full swing. Old Jem shook his head. Young Bart shook his fist. Middle-aged Martha, sex kitten turned animal protector, shook the box to make sure the stoat was still awake. Their glasses were drained-the stoat had a saucer-but Ephraim kept on drinking.

Old Jem led the leaving party, jabbing his stick in Ephraim's direction and muttering an ancient curse that had nothing to do with salt and vinegar crisps or pickled eggs.

The little old lady walked quietly to the bar, clutching her handbag under her arm and asked for a small, sweet sherry. She put an arm lock on Ephraim, the like of which he had not experienced since Aunt Lizzie caught him stealing a chocolate mouse off the Christmas tree.

"I believe you may be able to assist with my inquiries." Tears welled up as pain and embarrassment hurried him from the pub.

"Drink your cocoa while it's hot. No truth drug in there, I assure you" Miss Mardle gave him one of her sweetest smiles but it didn't make Ephraim feel any better. He knew the game was up.

"I must have your reasons for refusing to play the traditional role. Fraternising with the enemy at a time when Norfolk needs every friend to stay true ..." Her bony little knee came up sharply. He was winded but recovered quickly when she threatened to do it again.

"Orryte! Dunt yew keep a'layin' inter me ! I'm only flesh an' blud an' I carnt tearke ner more!"

Ephraim offered a full, contrite confession. The local constable arrived from Suffolk just after midnight. Miss Mardle made fresh cocoa.

Miss Mardle was given the freedom of Mayhem Parva. She was invited to open the church fete on the rectory lawn. Ephraim Edwards rediscovered his true self during week two at the corrective centre in South Pickenham.

He turned cantankerous or co-operative whenever he felt like it, with no moods in between. He pretended not to hear when given instructions by the guards but picked up casual chat from nearly a mile away if other inmates offered a twist of baccy or a Norwich City football season ticket for the latest information.

He swore at the governor in broad Norfolk, only to convince him seconds later that it was a famous blessing used by Queen Boadicea , Sir Thomas Browne, Lord Nelson, Jeremiah Colman, Sidney Grapes, Ron Saunders, Stephen Fry and Delia Smith at appropriate times.

Ephraim shunned food parcels from Clive the computer commuter. He spent hours in the exercise yard, shaking hands with an invisible holiday-maker ... "I remember yar nearme parfictly, but blowed if I kin think o'yar fearce" A wicked chortle proved the therapy was working.

The Four Ferrets was packed. Recent arrivals on the village scene mingled with holidaymakers. Clive, the computer commuter, organised a darts match. The landlord had to put on a fresh barrel of bitter.

Ephraim was extending the gnarled hand of Norfolk friendship to anyone lucky enough to find him with a half-filled tankard. He wore the regulation uniform of well-darned smock, battered trilby, shop-soiled buskins and hedging gloves.

He made a nominal charge for those obligatory photographs of Aunt Bessie on holiday bumping into one of the pub's rustic fixtures. He worked out special rates for those who wanted the services of Old Jem, Young Bart and Middle-aged Martha. The stoat came free.

Miss Mardle celebrated the successful completion of another tricky case with her favourite evening meal, Chicken Ding. The Chinese takeaway from Bamboo Curtains near the duckpond fitted snugly in the microwave.

Strange but warm... just like these people in rural Norfolk.

But how come most of them didn't talk a bit like all those rustic characters she had met in books and on television?

A minor consideration. The next big case beckoned in this part of the world where they tried to till enough common ground between yesterday's meadows and tomorrow's dual carriageways to make it interesting when they were all drawing pensions.

GET A GRIP

Teacher: "What are you making there, Johnny?"
Johnny: "Thass a portable, Miss."
Teacher: "A portable what?"
Johnny: "Dunno – so far I're only med the handle."

LESSON SEVENTEEN
PARISH PUMP

"If you want to keep your friends, stay off the parish council."

So runs the old adage, and there must be many a Norfolk village legend prepared to swear it carries the uncomfortable ring of truth.

I recall one rustic worthy from my early days on the local newspaper reporting rounds claiming he sought such high office merely to find out what the rest of the community really thought of him.

"They don't care if you have two wives, three fancy women and a posh mistress – but God help you if their footpaths, street lights and common grazing rights aren't sorted out properly!"

A commendable set of priorities, perhaps, in the eternal quest to keep rural life ticking over, but that parish councillor's colourful honesty betrayed masochistic tendencies beyond the call of duty.

"Someone has to do it" and "It's a challenge, I suppose" are the stock answers when you ask why anyone should bother to take on such a thankless task. With our villages changing so rapidly and so radically it can't be long before the minute book carries a health warning on the cover.

Events have taken savage turns in recent years. Parish councils, their virtues and faults jostling against apathy on their own doorsteps, are too often made to feel they're simply going through the motions of grass-roots democracy.

They weigh up local opinion –if it bothers to exist –and pass it on to a higher authority. In many cases, even where views are sincerely held and vehemently expressed, the result is a smart crack of the skull against a brick wall.

Some claim it has never been the same since the last reorganisation of local government, although I feel more allowances ought to be made for the reorganisation of Norfolk village life since those big changes took place in 1974.

In any event, it must be accepted that while parish councils may still be heard, they are having one heck of a job to get anyone to listen to them. Big Brother on the district and county councils – let alone the Grand Masters in Whitehall - is mocking Country Cousin.

Were the old rural district councils more in tune with village views and requirements? They served a different kind of Norfolk, but I am convinced many of those I saw and heard on Mitford and Launditch RDC business over four decades ago in the mid-Norfolk area would be staggered by the number of parish-pump protests being totally shunned these days.

Perhaps too many small communities are prepared to accept the current trend as inevitable ...they must know best on the next rung up the local government ladder ...and we are guilty of ignoring the system until something comes along to affect us. Like threats to close the village school, pub and post office or chopping the only bus service. Only then do we start thumping the tub and shouting about democratic rights.

If the parish council is to continue to form an important strand in the democratic pattern, we must treat it with more respect, not least at election time. This would set a much-needed good example to those who have the power either to implement village wishes or to provide a perfectly reasonable excuse for overriding them.

Let's give that old adage a fresh coat of paint:"If you value country life, look after your parish council."And that entails newcomers anxious to get involved doing it for the right reasons- not simply "stirring things up" or "leading this place out of the Dark Ages."

Parish politics can set back the cause of peaceful co-existence by 20 or 30 years every time a silly row spills over the pastoral scene, too easily tagged "old versus new."

Village stalwarts still relish the chance to pull rank in terms of service even if there's little scope for manoeuvre in the sort of arguments they used to share exclusively among themselves. Recent arrivals can be far too ready to feel unloved, unwanted and unappreciated despite the wealth of experience and vision they are capable of offering.

The true art is for the newcomer to come up with a cracking idea and then convince the hard-baked local it was his magnificent ruse after all. In turn, the thoughtful local can credit his new-found friend with providing just the right kind of inspiration and backing for such a far-seeing and mutually beneficial suggestion.

Honour satisfied on both sides, with that brand of intelligent co-operation vital to impress Big Brother... or even Grand Master.

Another useful tip for those determined to take up Norfolk rural cudgels. Make sure you know the difference between the Parish Council and the Parochial Church Council before you start criticising the village envelope plan or insulting the vicar.

Remarkably enough, the popular BBC Television comedy show starring Dawn French as the Vicar of Dibley regularly managed to confuse these two august bodies. It made me wonder if the scriptwriters, actors and producer really knew what goes on in a country community.

They may have fallen prey to one of those glossy magazines selling countryside images by the hundredweight to avid readers in town and city. Lunch al fresco, William Morris wallpaper in the dining room, best spot for the hammock beyond the vegetable patch, how to buy a pony, how to restore a derelict corn mill and where to hang a nineteenth century Hindu Pashwar cloth.

All purposeful strands in the big debate about where the countryside is going and if one is inclined to go with it. Does one have to accept that village life is becoming an adjunct of smart urban life rather than something able to fly the flag of independence?

Perhaps if we all went back to individually hand-plucking our chickens the world would be a better place. It would help to ignore these sorts of lurid lines from twee journalists: "Norfolk has remained rooted in the 1950s as long as it had the choice. The samphire grass produces its stalky asparagus for headscarfed figures to gather in as a summer delicacy, and the crab pots bulge enough to keep the stalls covered and the fishermen happy. Gnarled oysters, sold behind the tractor wheels, still cost a fraction of the London price."

Ah, the world is your tractor as you take a peek at that quaint backside sticking out brazenly into the old German Ocean...

"But Norfolk no longer has a choice. Its beauty lies in its faults. Both are being discovered by people in search of rural bliss. Houses in counties further south and west have become so expensive that these bleak wastes have developed a certain cachet for home hunters."

Be honest, you are beginning to suspect that this writer – George Borrow meets Barbara Cartland on a windswept marsh –might have Norfolk sussed. Here comes the knockout punch... .

"Now that the drawbridge is down, there's no sparing the rest of Norfolk." A truly chilling sentence delivered, it seems, with a throaty metropolitan cackle. "You thought you were beyond all this, my fine rustic friends, but you might as well accept your fate along with all the rest. Don't ring us. We'll come to see you."

The article, complete with a list of recommended estate agents to fend off criticism about being too sentimental, concluded Norfolk was no longer on the way to nowhere. The game was up. Those tatty old folders marked "Isolation", "Insulation" and "Indigenous Idiosyncrasies " would soon be replaced by a file on newcomers worth knowing, even if they were gripped by a myth of bygone rural England.

Well, that was in 1988.Norfolk replied that when the first reasonable missionaries came trundling over the sugar beet fields, the peasants held their fire, listened and accepted new-fangled gifts like electricity, mains sewerage, indoor bathrooms, insecticides and instructions on how to board up inglenook fireplaces.

Then we began to realise that a little civilisation could be a dangerous thing. New chiefs spoke with forked tongues. They shut down our railways, closed our village pubs, schools and shops, ripped out our hedges, covered our oak beams with hideous floral wallpaper and told us country people were the last people to be entrusted with the countryside.

Just as we showed signs of coming to terms with that brave new Norfolk designed with some of our strange little habits in mind –like talking to each other in pubs until the next round was due – along came the winebar whizzkid mentality to urge us towards a better understanding of commuters and booming property prices.

Now , as Norfolk refuses to fall in with even more lurid glossy magazine images, the old guard who built the drawbridge and the inspired battalion of newcomers who help to man it, say they simply do not want the forced excitement, the artificial expansion, the short-term thinking, the fast-buck philosophy, that goes with an exercise built largely on greed.

Norfolk could easily choke on the slice of cake so many still seem determined to stuff down its throat.

SAME AGAIN

Posh visitor to donkey man on Yarmouth beach: "I say, what do your beautiful creatures have for lunch?"
  Donkey man: "Searme as us – 'bowt 40 minnits."

LESSON EIGHTEEN
SMILING THROUGH

Elder son was about four and just feeling his comedy feet when he banged on the toilet door.

"Go away," I growled, "I'm busy."

"But Dad, I've got ever such an important question to ask you..." The little pleader persisted until granted an audience.

"Come on then, what is it that can't wait a moment longer?" I struggled for dignity as he shuffled towards me to ensure full attention was being paid.

With a searching stare and confidential pose way beyond his years, he gently intoned: "The old days were the best, weren't they, Dad?"

He didn't hang about for an answer but raced across the landing chortling loudly. I sat wondering what on earth we had unleashed on an unsuspecting Norfolk before half a smile of admiration crossed my lips.

Perhaps I had cited "the good old days" once or twice but there had been no obvious evidence of such rousing recall making a strong impression on so young and tender a mind.

Now I had to change tack swiftly, if only to prevent further inroads into a proud reputation as a thoroughly modern father and husband with no delusions about the recent past.

That little domestic interlude still comes out to play should I lapse into any "now, when I was a lad" comparisons. Happily, my sons now yield to nostalgia occasionally when I try to tell them off.

"But we used to do that all the while when we were very young and you never said anything. Why is it wrong now?"

"Because it is and you ought to know better! If I'd answered my parents back like you do, well, it would have been a ding o'the lug and straight to bed with no tea at the very least..."

The generation game may have more to do with fun than fury, but it's still worth playing when the comparatively young ask too many questions and ignore too many answers.

My "golden age" was the 1950s as I grew up in mid-Norfolk, one of a family of 10 children at the heart of an agricultural community. The world was smaller, slower, quieter, kinder – and occasionally more pungent when the honeycart came round. While my boys text friends to find out if their fathers ever fall prey to rampant nostalgia, let me set the survey ball rolling with 10 things about yesterday that were infinitely better than today:

1. Social behaviour – people were generally more polite and friendly, and elders respected.
2. Healthy eating – home-grown vegetables and free-range poultry flourished.
3. Village shops – there were more, serving important social as well as economic needs.
4. Rural transport- it offered plenty of encouragement for folk to walk or ride bikes.
5. Sex education – birds, bees, cows, mares, stallions ... no need for lectures.
6. Popular music – most songs had recognisable tunes and you could hear the words.
7. Entertainment – mainly homespun fun before television took control of countless lives.
8. Crime and punishment – the truly local bobby did much to nip potential trouble in the bud.
9. The environment – lengthmen looked after roads, ditches and hedges. Proper care of the community
10. Quality of life – simplicity (not to be confused with ignorance) is a virtue too often cherished only after it has disappeared.

LOADED DICE

Still wondering what to buy as a festive gift for that special person in your life? I may be able to help.

My new board game, Drawbridge (patent applied for), should be in the shops at least a week before Christmas. It is designed to bring some of Norfolk's growing problems into sharper focus around the family hearth.

Aim of the game is to build as few new homes as possible on a journey across the county, a journey fraught with dangers for all concerned.

Perhaps a few will hear echoes of other well-loved board games in certain instructions, such as "Do not pass Hoe" and "Go directly to Bale", but this is the first to be specifically targeted at a rural resistance movement.

Those with a sound knowledge of local geography, including the location and destination of all by-roads, must be ahead of the race when it comes to avoiding dangerous spots like Very Long Stratton, Mortar-on-the-Hill, Thorpe Endless, Burston-at-Seams, Shotesham-in-the-Foot, Stoke Wholly Wild, Kelling Fields, Thirty Mile Bank, Etling Brown and Fedupton-with Fishley.

Naturally "planning gains", occasionally known as bare-faced bribes, proliferate as players reach quieter corners like Sloley and Limpenhoe, but heavy penalties are sure to follow acceptance of a new library or doctors' surgery in exchange for permission to put up 120 executive dwellings on a one-acre plot.

Other developments along the way include:
• Landing on a concrete mixer or theodolite means going back to the start to attend a public inquiry into the Structure Plan.
• Throwing a six forces you to miss a go in order to read another White Paper on the future of rural communities.
• Settling on any water tap in the first 20 squares brings an extra throw to ensure supplies direct from aquifers and rivers.
• Alighting on a brownfield site heralds a Campaign for the Protection of Rural England reward of moving on 12 places or collecting your first hard hat. Three of these can be exchanged for a dumper truck, six for a mechanical digger.
• If you are fortunate enough to land on the Fortress Norfolk square, and your local roots go back at least five generations, you can ignore all inducements and penalties on the route to the finish.
• If you are unlucky enough to land on the Fortress Norfolk square and you cannot pronounce Hargham, Hautbois and Happisburgh, you must take out life membership with the National House Builders' Federation.

Yes, this new game is marginally biased in favour of native participants, but surely that makes a pleasant change from having the dice loaded against them during decades of rules being handed down from Westminster and Whitehall.

Drawbridge is defiantly home-grown. Get it for a loved-one this festive season and build a better relationship.

PLOT THICKENS

I looked at my vegetable plot the other day, turned it over in my mind and decided to leave well alone.

Well, not so much a plot as a flimsy outline for the first chapter of a story unlikely to be written this century. But I can live with weeds, sloth and guilt.

Even after a country upbringing knee-deep in home-grown potatoes, peas, brussel sprouts, cabbages, parsnips, carrots, radishes and beans – and that was just one side of the old family seat – I tend to leave garden glories to others.

March sunshine sets off an alarm: "This is your early morning call to start cleaning up your act. The fork is that implement with sharp bits at the end of a long handle covered in cobwebs behind 27 cardboard boxes in the washroom..."

Sadly, the wind changes and brings 36 hours of much-needed rain to curb burgeoning ambitions. Then, only minutes after a return to blue skies and favourable forecasts, old back trouble strikes as you stretch for a growing manual on the top shelf.

Twinges of regret. The plot thickens with everybody else in a six-hectare radius digging, dibbling (I know all the technical terms) and dehydrating.

Pangs of remorse. With wife and sons spotted with machete, mosquito net and malevolent grins through the study window.

Still, I can hack it through the jungle of recriminations, bolstered by memories of brave folk at village chapel harvest festivals many trenches ago. The mid-week sale of produce after Sunday's services certainly sorted the winning wheat from the churlish chaff.

"Who'll bid me a shilling for a jar of Mildred's wonderful home-made chutney? A tanner for these champion onions from Eric's garden? Two bob for this golden sheaf of home-made bread straight from Mary's wall oven?"

It could have been so socially divisive, setting green-fingered parishioner against ham-fisted neighbour in the shadow of the pulpit.

But the coulds and the could- nots, the doers and the dawdlers, the quick and the dead-slows, they accepted all the differences with good grace, took variety as the spice of country life and helped me grow up without much of a complex about playing such a small role every seed-time and harvest.

I can live with weeds, sloth and guilt – but I do admire those who don't. At least I don't have the vicar peering over my fence to prompt one of the best cultivated responses in Norfolk horticultural folklore:

"My goodness, what a splendid job you and the Lord have done in that garden!"

"Ah, so that might be – but yew should a'sin what a mess that wuz when the Lord had it orl on his own!"

DECIMAL POINT

I was dispensing a few of Aunt Agatha's priceless philosophical gems at a village harvest supper the other night when the penny dropped.

"A thipenny bit ent so good as a sixpence, thow that go ter church more often." As I slipped that one into the Norfolk collection box I realised there were several present who could be forgiven for missing the point.

We who made our first hundred before Monday, 15 February 1971 tend to assume everyone remembers threepenny pieces, tanners, shillings, florins, half-crowns and ten-bob notes. We are bilingual when it comes to currency, daring ourselves to convert back into old money whenever we want a reminder of how prices have soared.

The fact it's so long since we went decimal makes no difference to this twin-track approach to financial considerations. We share a single currency but still add up or take away at the double.

I recall a significant pointer to such aversion to change. As we squared up to the challenge of D-Day, 1971 a dear old Norfolk traditionalist who had more in common with Brockdish than Brussels hinted the revolution should have been delayed.

"They might he' waited till all the old people had died," she opined as drums banged, bunting flew and we bid a fond adieu to 12 pennies in a shilling.

The little burst of Norfolk defiance came back to me with a letter from the Rev. Ron Astin of Overstrand. His wife was collecting money at a Mothers' Union meeting in Sheringham just after decimal coinage was introduced. An elderly member offered an upheld purse with the words: "You tearke it. I dunt unnerstand this new munny". As Mrs Astin refused to take money from the purse, the old lady continued: "I hent bin a'shoppin' since this new munny cum in an' I arnt gowin' tew while that larst!"

PS Aunt Agatha she say – Thass a pity we carnt live in the parst ... that'd be so much cheaper.

SUNNY SURVEY

You know what some people say about statistics...

Well, the charabanc-load delivered in the summer of 2004 by the East of England Tourist Board deserves some sort of measured response.

Trouble is, you can't argue about most figures connected with tourism's apparent emergence as Norfolk's number one industry – simply because they are too big.

How can you possibly disprove that it's worth about £2m a year to the county? Or that 4.6m people came to stay here in 2002 and there were another 45m day trips to local attractions? Plenty of other king-sized numbers to back the case for being top of the economy charts and supporting 55.000 jobs. And a trumpet call from Crispian Emberson, director of Norfolk Tourism: "It is essential that everyone concerned continues to support its development."

I'm a bit concerned, Crispian, as a proud native and long-term resident of the North Norfolk coast. For a start, when will you know we have reached saturation point?

If your researchers who specialise in compiling statistics while on holiday (naturally) in the fairest county of them all want a few worth-while diversions, let me proffer figures they must not ignore.

In the interests of fairness and balance, qualities attracting so many to Norfolk for holidays or to put down full-time roots, I conducted a completely impartial survey on and around Cromer's bustling streets and seafront.

I couldn't reach as many locals as I would have liked as 73% prefer to stay out of sight until October, and a few visitors claimed they couldn't understand what I was on about.

Here's what tourism can mean to Cromer on one hot afternoon in summer:

Average journey by car through the town centre provided 967 drivers with a perfect chance to catch up with holiday reading.

Of these drivers, 54 also found time to buy new books along the way – and 11 joined the local library service.

A total of 1794 people struck up friendships while waiting to cross the road. On one especially busy corner there were nine reunions, four proposals of marriage, three trial separations, two natural births and one irretrievable breakdown.

Out of 30 local businesses questioned, all said there were plenty of people about. But they were invariably suffering from a common Norfolk affliction... "They ent spendin' noffin."

Of 642 visitors carrying fish and chips, 96% preferred eating them outside, with seats overlooking the promenade and pier a favourite spot. Nearly 700 plump seagulls and starlings said they approved of tourism in general.

The Cromer Pier regeneration programme was applauded by all but two of 1500 people interviewed. One complained he couldn't get a signal on his mobile phone. The other complained that he could – and he'd come on holiday from Aberdeen for "a wee bit o'peace and quiet".

Just under 82% of visitors on the seafront said they felt obliged to try Cromer crabs during their stay. "You wouldn't leave Heacham without a sprig of lavender or Sidestrand without a poppy!" proclaimed one woman.

A cynical 14% refused to answer any questions, claiming it was possible to twist replies to suit any cause. One said: "We take all statistics with a pinch of salt, a drop of vinegar, a drizzle of butter and a bunch of samphire."

SQUIT TRAVELS

I caught echoes of a welcome cultural exchange on entering one of my favourite village watering-holes the other evening.

"You should have been here last night," said the landlord, a true son of Norfolk who loves to tease as he pulls the pumps and turns on the gossip taps.

Evidently, somebody had expressed surprise that more than one local knew 'slantendicular' meant not quite straight.

Just one of our dialect delights, in fact, to cover such a state of affairs. 'On the sosh' and 'on the huh' do just as good a job.

This set us mardling about other Norfolk words and expressions that share equal billing among those determined to keep them in circulation.

I settled on 'puckaterry', meaning muddle, confusion and distress and probably a derivative of purgatory.

"Oh, you mean all of a muckwash!" exclaimed mine amiable host.

I moved on to 'harriage', from the same department, clearly coming from harry – to harass or lay waste.

"Gone to harriage' is gone to rack and ruin. There have been efforts to tie it all up with the place Harwich, but there's no proven connection.

There's an obvious danger in claiming certain words as exclusively our own.

Even 'squit', Norfolk's most precious commodity, entertaining nonsense, is known and used in the dialect of Herefordshire... a fair way from God's Own Acre.

I looked up the word in Robert Forby's Vocabulary of East Anglia, first published in 1830 but still the dialect bible for a host of enthusiasts.

"A word of supreme contempt for a very diminutive person – 'a paltry squit!' In Old English it was 'squib', but that word seems to be lost, and the more is the pity, for at any rate it was less offensively contemptuous."

So 'squit' as we know and love it today meant something else round here not too far back. The Oxford English Dictionary includes it as small insignificant person in the same sense as 'squirt', although my Reader's Digest Oxford Complete Wordfinder also offers the dialect meaning of nonsense.

Just for fun, I turned to a glossary of the Dorset dialect compiled by that wonderful poet William Barnes in 1886. There I found 'squit' meaning to make a very slight sound and 'squitters' included as the diarrhoea in cattle.

ROMANTIC DUO

Is the age of romance over in Norfolk? Or can hearts still be set a'fluttering by a coy wink, a billet-doux in local dialect or a surprise bunch of nasturtiums? Bluff bachelors Art and Doc salty veterans of the Morston and District Matchmaking Society and Stiffkey Tea Dance Club, offer a few thoughts on the bill and coo situation:

Art – When did you start going out with girls?
Doc – When I found out they weren't boys.
Art – Didn't your first love go for the quiet things in life?
Doc – Yes, like the folding of a ten-bob note.
Art – I found out my first date was being unfaithful to me
Doc – Did she talk to strange men?
Art – No, but she had a nasty habit of listening.
Doc – Girls from Langham used to chase me. They'd through flowers at my feet. They'd fall at my feet. They worshipped at my feet. They didn't go much on my face, but my feet were having a wonderful time.
Art – I took a girl home once, and do you know what she said?
Doc – No.
Art – That's right. So I smiled at her big sister.
Doc – What followed?
Art – I did. Being a lady she dropped her eyelids. Being a gentleman, I picked them up again on the road to Binham.
Doc – I remember her. You parted on the 35th anniversary of her 21st birthday.
Art - Better than that one you called Echo because she always had the last word.
Doc – Still, we haven't lost our touch after all these years. And Norfolk mawthers are best.
Art – Yes, you can always tell a Norfolk mawther...
Doc – But you can't tell her much!

TRENDY CRABLAND

That's the trouble with experts. Too many of them. They can finish up contradicting each other and confusing us.

I was all set to break the habits of a lifetime and contemplate the future while climate boffins pointed to this part of the world as an even bigger magnet for holidaymakers.

Yes, dear old Cromer could help put Mediterranean hordes in the shade from the 2020s with just the right sort of temperatures for sun-seekers.

And if the pier and promenade should overflow, Sunny Hunny and Yummy Yarmouth would be geared for extra rations.

An exciting vision of Costa del Crabland, with gambling dens, trendy nightclubs, yachting marinas, drive-in hypermarkets and special weekend breaks for the under-80s put an extra spring into my daily blow along the clifftops.

Why shouldn't North Norfolk enjoy a slice of this freshly-baked tourism cake? Poppyland has gone to seed. Let's have Boppyland for tireless dancers, Floppyland for tired businessmen, Jaloppyland for customised car fanatics and Stroppyland for frustrated football supporters and local councillors who want to let off steam.

I warmed to my role as a marketing guru. Cromer's brand new image had to spread rapidly either way along the coast.

The Cliffhanger Casino at Trimingham caught my eye, complete with towering apartments billed as "affordable housing – if you win every night."

The Elephant Experience theme park at West Runton caught my ear, complete with trumpeting bays billed as "alternative hunting – form you own tusk force."

The Clement Scott Discotheque at Overstrand caught my imagination, complete with thumping amplifiers billed as "loud enough to put the wind up Black Shuck."

The Garden of Sleep Takeaway at Sidestrand caught my nostrils, complete with local delicacies billed as 'sinkers and swimmers for the more mature palate'.

Such tantalising attractions on the horizon with experts reminding us how development might be swift given the right economic and planning conditions. Remember, the Costas 40 years ago were just a cluster of boring fishing villages.

Enter another climate specialist licensed to spill cold water over seaside dreams.

He calls for a ban on any new development in the zone at risk from coastal erosion in the next 50 years.

What a spoilsport! Just as I get dewy-eyed over tomorrow for the first time in years I'm forced into the idea of managed realignment.

I trundle back to the Elastic Stocking Tearooms, ask for the heating to be turned up and realise I still live on the Costa del Uusion.

Briefly, that adventurous mood flickers again as a retired bingo caller drops in to chat about the good old days of full houses and decent prizes.

He wonders out load what odds he could get against the Cliffhanger Casino in Trimingham being built before it tumbles into the sea.

A lady behind the urn says it's all being taken care of in the "daft shoreline management plan". No, she doesn't mean 'draft'.

And would we please close the door so she can avoid one coming straight in from the UEA Climate Research Unit.

DAILY CHRONICLE
I have a stock answer ready whenever my sons turn cheeky and ask what I did in the war.

"Well, I slept through most of what was left after my arrival hastened its end," is a perfectly legitimate counter from anyone born in 1944.

They still seem surprised that my earliest memories do not feature doo-dlebugs, gas masks and air-raid shelters. I remind them how little they recall of their opening months.

Elder lad cannot remember Norwich City topping the old Division One table shortly after he was born in September, 1986. Nor can he bring to mind a University of East Anglia survey suggesting job hunters over the age of 35 were virtually on the scrapheap.

Younger son has no recollection of the county's first outbreak of the virulent sugar been disease rhizomania a few days after he turned up in October, 1989. And Kazuo Ishiguro's Booker Prize victory with *Remains of the Day* passed him by completely. The big consolation is on the shelves of my study. Every day of their lives so far has been chronicled in detail with special emphasis on the Norfolk world around them.

While such an exercise may leave them less than enthusiastic to follow suit in careful joined-up writing, they accept how Aged P's daily diary habit could provide useful background information for various projects as well as cast light on family fortunes.

When such benevolence is in the air, I push my familiar text about our past feeding the future, yesterday helping make some sense of today and tomorrow. I've reached that time of life when little bits of my past insist on lining up for inspection. That can lead to more laments than approval, more sighs than applause, but some events present an unashamedly warm glow.

While much of the nation was concerned with poignant VE Day cele-brations I headed for Swaffham and the annual reunion of Old Hamondians. Out of nowhere stepped Keith Whitesides to remind me how we sat next to each other on our first day at grammar school in 1955.

More vibrant echoes at Holt Farmers' Club annual dinner when I told a few yarns from my rural childhood." You knew two of my uncles, Dick and Mark Flood," smiled Roger Long. That encouraged a lengthy caval-cade of characters.

Just to prove I can move bang up to date when it comes to pop music, I tapped my good foot incessantly as Shawaddywaddy let rip at the National Association of Estate Agents' presidential ball.

Local lad Chris hall from Skeyton was installed in the top post. I sang for my supper – and had to admit I knew all the words to You've Got What It Takes and Under The Moon of Love.

Nostalgia set to music is a potent force. And it doesn't end with We'll Meet Again.

SEVEN IN A ROW

I don't gamble as a rule – and it's odds-on against another Fakenham flutter without serious advice from a proven stayer in the tipping stakes.

My bank manager and a coterie of financial friends, perhaps anticipating a cheap laugh on a sunny afternoon, extended a cordial invitation to join them in the search for racing certainties.

Their hospitality hinted at compassion on the eve of calamity. It could have been the way I sweated up before the 1.40 or lost my way to the start of the 2.15. Maybe I would have done better without blinkers.

In any event, my real handicap soon came trundling down the home straight. I couldn't find a winner in seven races. A couple of seconds, yes, but no good without an each-way bet behind them.

Walcot Lad was one of those runners-up, a selection inspired more by Norfolk coastal village name association than any data from the form-book. "Did he hit the wall?" smirked one of the banking fraternity. A few more sure-fire choices followed suit, refusing to rise to the occasion and then asking for several more fences to be taken into consideration.

I crept out of the loser's enclosure without calling for a steward's inquiry – I didn't fancy a dope test – and prepared my podium speech for the wife...

"Do you know, dear, I went right through the card!

"Seven in a row. That's consistency for you. They want me on the board of the IMF."

She suspected that might stand for I'm Maintaining Fakenham.

SHEET LIGHTNING

Did you hear about the Norfolk inventor who dismantled his microwave oven and then set it up at the foot of his bed?

Well, he now gets 12 hours sleep in under five minutes.

LESSON NINETEEN
MOVE WITH THE TIMES?

One of Norfolk's most endearing habits is to pay homage to all latest fads, to embrace the true spirit of progress in which they are wrapped – and then quietly shuffle along the same old homely track.

Self-delusion? More like a shrewd tactic at the heart of a self-preservation programme unlikely to be wrecked by a change of digit at the start of the year.

Yes, there will be renewed demands to move with the times, voiced mostly by those with vested interests in items Norfolk could well do without. Like motorways, more mobile phones, mass tourism projects and towering, glowering masts mucking up our glorious skylines.

No, we must not buckle under torrents of jibes about living in the past, ignoring the "harsh economic realities" of a changing world and frightening off generous developers who have nothing but our future betterment in mind.

Maybe it will get harder to trick the prophets of boom into thinking we are with them all the way, but I offer a wish list designed to bring long-term comfort and joy to an area still envied for being different.

Jealous protection of that reputation is the main motive behind these fervent hopes:

Stop paying lip service to the idea of public transport and use it whenever possible. There's no shame in being seen on a bus or train even if you do have a smart new car.

Take a closer interest in local affairs, and not just when an issue affects you. Councillors, officers and MPS should be held to regular account.

Encourage children to feel more at home in the countryside instead of using it simply as an escape from urban tedium. "What's that crop over there?" is a good starting point.

Talk to your neighbours, even if it's only to tell them how the internet puts you in touch with the other side of the world. Communications still begin at home.

Stay cool in congested corners, especially during the holiday season. Remember how pavement niggle and pub bar nudge can breed nasty things like road rage.

Never be ashamed of your Norfolk accent if you are luck enough to have one. Twaddle about "received pronunciation" comes mainly from grey armies elsewhere.

Ignore all surveys pointing to Norfolk as one of the safest, healthiest, quietest and cheapest places to live. Stating the obvious can entice exploitation.

Beware all who claim far-reaching alterations will affect them as much as you, for good or for bad. Tell them dewin' diffrunt can mean leaving well alone.

ON THE FARM

I know several folk who own up to deep feelings of unease as they enter Norfolk's Rural Life Museum at Gressenhall.

Echoes of the old workhouse follow them around like paupers seeking grains of charity to lift bleak lives.

Perhaps sharp contrasts with a world of comparative affluence left behind for an hour or two breed a strange brand of guilt.

Our family visit the other day left me with a new kind of sadness – and not all of it tied up in a grudging admission that many farming items on display figured in my childhood world a few furrows away at Beeston.

It was the manner in which children were being chaperoned around Union Farm over the road that mocked my harvest holiday memories.

Where we were allowed to discover for ourselves the wonders of field and farm, hedgerow and headland, today's youngsters are tethered to a tight leash. Mainly for safety's sake we are told.

It is a proper working farm with rare breeds, the Norfolk Four-Course Rotation and walks alongside riverside meadows among the attractions, with a cart-ride into the recent past for good measure.

Obviously there were holidaymakers from urban parts, but I noted several Norfolk children doing the rounds.

It became clear some were being introduced to pigs, goats, cows, sheep, geese and hens for the first time.

Yes, this is much better than no farmyard experience at all, but how strange it has to be packaged for local consumption in the middle of a county proudly built on agriculture. It is not to long ago when Norfolk laughed at evacuees who rushed to tell the farmer his horse was losing its petrol.

PLANNING PLOYS

I have long enjoyed lively sparring sessions with some of the key characters involved in determining Norfolk's fate.

Planners must have thick skins, ready smiles, reasonable answers, useful alibis and a working knowledge of how life ticked over quite pleasantly, thank you, before they came along.

Most of them helping prepare us for the challenges of a new age arrived here on a wave of missionary zeal, ready to light up the road to nowhere with glowing texts from more sophisticated parts.

This blatant emphasis on hauling a backward Norfolk into line rather than applauding the supporting a deep-felt desire to carry on being different has provoked fiercest debate during he past 30 years or so.

To be fair, the argument would have been even more lopsided without the genial and passionate presence of John Ayton as head of planning at County Hall. Proud of his home-grown roots, he told me many times that planners did more than most to maintain Norfolk's unique identity.

"Planners do not create development pressures; they try to advise planning authorities on how to cope with them" he stressed in a letter to me after I had launched an outspoken attack on him and his like.

That line jumped out for fresh inspection a few days ago when poor old Dereham had to face up to even more threats of over-development. Mayor Chris Thorne hit out at an application to Breckland Council for 96 homes off Dunlop Road. "We are totally against building more homes in the town until the infrastructure catches up," he said.

He must have been looking for a measure of support, or even a spot of useful advice, from council officers. Some hopes! Breckland planning man Nick Moys admitted the size of the application merited considerable thought. – "but all we can consider are details of the plans; it is not for us to say whether or not there should be no more housing."

Could he not offer a view without compromising his role? Is he not aware of the amount of disquiet in Dereham over excessive development? In what circumstances would he and his colleagues feel obliged to give an opinion?

Just compare this current Breckland reluctance to get involved to a North Norfolk blast from the not-too-distant past when planners were freely cast as unashamed backers of the prophets of boom.

In September 1988 Brian Murphy, North Norfolk's chief planning officer, criticised members of the district council's development committee for ignoring advice (from planning officers) by approving plans for new houses in open countryside rather than within villages.

"I really am very concerned. The way it has been going in the last few meetings is really quite environmentally disastrous. You are going quite badly wrong in relation to policy. I have the task of trying to preserve the character of North Norfolk, and this is ruinous."

Murphy's Law. Ayton's advice. Seems we could do with a few examples from a decade or two ago to boost present campaigns against speculators and spoilers. Planners might not always be right. I maintain they should speak out when something is undeniably wrong.

RABBIT TALES

Rabbit pie and jugged hare used to be familiar items on our Norfolk menu, especially at the time of year when the corn harvest boosted the culinary crop.

Sadly, the introduction of myxomatosis in the 1950s put me and many others completely off the idea of eating rabbit meat again.

This disease, brought in deliberately, caused the death of countless animals. It was painful to see them with their heads swollen to twice the normal size and their eyes closed.

They suffered at the side of roads as I biked past on my way to school, often pretending not to notice them. Part of our staple family diet disappeared. Although new generations flourished after the epidemic, we simply could not stomach rabbit at the meal table.

I was set off down this trail by a letter from Bert Miller of Horsham St Faith. He recalled "an annual event in a boy's life in the late 1920s when a lad with the much-treasured shut knife became very popular."

Bert refers to the Norfolk words "hulk", to skin and gut a rabbit, and "huddle", to pass the leg of a rabbit through the sinews of the other to enable it to be carried easily.

I must admit to being conspicuous by my absence when these practices were employed in our locality before myxomatosis. Despite a country upbringing, I was most squeamish about the preparation of certain foods.

You wouldn't have found me in Elizabeth Harland's kitchen as she sorted out an old recipe mentioned in her book, No Halt at Sunset, The Diary of a Country Housewife, first published in 1951:

"First cut up a rabbit, boil in vegetable soup until tender. Put meat twice through mincer, then put into saucepan, add quarter pound of butter (margarine), a chopped onion, salt and pepper if necessary, a teaspoon of paprika. Mix in a little of the liquid to which a little gelatine has been added, put in a long mould, place in fridge to set. Eat cold, cut in small slices."

Norfolk dialect words for a hare include Sally, Sarah and Sukey. There's scope for confusion when it comes to "bunny", our dialect word for a bruise or swelling, and "rabbit", which in carpentry means to rebate or cut grooves.

PENSION POWER

While splinters multiply as you slide down the banister of life, remember wise words you heard on the landing of youth.

That's an old Norfolk proverb I just made up to partner telling echoes from my farmyard world of over 50 years ago.

I was muttering and moaning about the iniquities of a system which demanded dirty hands and aching limbs in return for a few coppers.

The Saturday job was getting me down. I scowled at cattle snorting for feed, chickens itching to be cleaned out and pigs spoiling for another rough-and-tumble over pails of swill.

I kicked at the chaff-cutter, cursed the pain shooting through my toes and asked my ancient minder why such mundane tasks survived into the middle of the twentieth century. His smile and response shamed me with their gentle reproach.

"Come on, bor. Try and enjoy yarself now... these here are the good ole days yew'll talk abowt later on!"

He was right, of course, and probably had been offered the selfsame advice by another Norfolk son of the soil many years before. The sort of homely wisdom worth handing down whenever rebellious youth threatens to veer out of control.

I was upbraided more than once by our parish elders before leaving school and discovering they really did know a few things about life and its little vagaries. Thankfully, there were opportunities to go back with a dash of gratitude and humility.

Yes, I am a touch sentimental about my rural roots, but certain points about closely-knit and predominantly self-sufficient communities of a half a century ago need emphasising whenever grandiose schemes to "revive country life" are mooted.

One of the latest signals £2.5m of Millennium Commission money for Help the Aged to "release the huge potential" of retired folk living in rural areas. As 20% of Norfolk's population is made up of pensioners, double the national average, this county was bound to feature strongly in early reckoning.

We are treated to clever labels like "Pension Power", "Grey Grit" and the "Wrinkly Revolution", and I suppose they make a welcome change from "the most vulnerable members of society", a phrase beloved of patronising politicians.

Frankly, though, I consider it a bit of an insult to suggest that Norfolk's growing army of retired workers need big financial incentives and a blaze of publicity to use their skills, enthusiasm and years of experience to benefit places where they live.

The process, a perfectly natural one, is well established on a vibrant and voluntary basis in many country areas, especially on the village hall beat. I see the exciting and galvanising effects on my regular rounds up and down the county.

Newcomers, often worldly-wise, articulate and self-assured, can set examples without putting on a blatant air of superiority. (The heavy-handed approach simply leads from irritation to isolation) And it is from the retired ranks that most of the solid support comes.

Native ancient minders may be thinner in the ground, but even the first years of a new millennium have to inspire a few of the good old days we'll talk about later on.

Some might dress them up and put it down to a new social network – but I reckon mardling and mucking-in with remain the real benefactors.

CLASS ACCENTS

There are moments designed to send the native spirit soaring above the monotonous rooftops of Norfolk "progress".

One such moment blessed my visit to Scarning, a fast-spreading community leaving little to nature or the imagination on Dereham's western fringes.

The village primary school, down to 17 pupils not long ago, has wheeled in extra mobile classrooms to cope with a dramatic surge at the heart of the county.

Proof, perhaps, that every "crowd" might carry a silver lining...

I accepted an invitation from teacher Philip Brazier to prepare a lesson on Norfolk dialect for years four and five. They showed me the extent of recent language studies – I followed a New Zealander and a Dutch girl into the school spotlight – while their general knowledge of local words and expressions warmed the "Stewkey" Blues (cockles) of my heart.

Then for that golden parting-shot from a lad who immediately raised his hand when I asked why dialects are important. "Because that would be very boring if we all sounded the same," he beamed, as if anticipating my warmest approval.

The need for colour and individuality in the face of a relentless tide of change and uniformity is at the heart of a campaign to preserve and promote our vernacular, a campaign given fresh impetus and direction by the formation of Friends Of Norfolk Dialect in 1999. (Visit the website www.norfolkdialect.com)

Obviously, it is vital to steer that crusade into schools, where a crammed curriculum leaves little scope for the glories of squit, trosh and tricolate.

It is largely due to the enlightened enthusiasm of individual teachers that the "proper" sound of Norfolk is being heard.

LUDDITE LABEL

I celebrated another birthday at the weekend, paying no heed to insensitive souls suggesting it was time to start counting backwards.

Just for fun, I looked up a few episodes from history coinciding with my special date. As one yet to experience complete ease at the cutting edge of modern technology, I found a certain empathy with events of 1811.

Civil disturbances in England's hosiery industry, known as the Luddite riots, first broke out in Nottingham. Bands of unemployed workers began smashing machines, moving from town to town and vowing revenge on those whose innovations had left them penniless and their families starving.

The riots, which really put the wind up the establishment, did not abate until October 1816. Technology marched on. The Industrial Revolution proved a mightier force than mobs waging guerrilla war in the workshops.

I still use pen and ink. I shun mobile phones. I have a big collection of vinyl records. I look things up in books. I do not drive a car. I cannot set the video recorder. I occasionally glory in my so-called incompetence.

It is most unlikely that I will ever catch up, but like an old horseman confronted by a gleaming new tractor, I sense the world keeps moving on. Not going with it can be interpreted as sheer cussedness, but there's no need to take it further than that.

The "Luddite" label seems to be stuck on anyone who dares resist the latest trends or questions the obvious differences between torrents of information and genuine knowledge or phoney contact and sincere communication.

We older lads at the cutting edge of common sense ought to be praised instead of pilloried. Perhaps we Pisceans should prepare to lead the charge to smash a few dangerous myths outside the hosiery trade.

"At their best, Pisceans are receptive, compassionate, understanding, idealistic, refined, gentle, loyal, sensitive, artistic and mystical..."

I blush at so accurate a summary in my special birthday book. But wait, this extra bit must have come over the internet down at the cyber cafe while I wasn't looking. "On the negative side, they can be over-emotional, impractical, self-indulgent, indecisive, vague, moody, unstable, despondent..."

I did have an off-day in 1985. I threw a little wobbly when the Test cricket moved to Talk Radio. I may have wavered in support of alternative energy sources when the Swaffham wind turbine reminded me I couldn't stand heights. I wept at the thought of even more of dear old Norfolk disappearing under bricks and mortar. I laughed out loud as balloons of political pomposity were pricked before our very eyes.

There we are, a curious mixture - an average sort of chap. Don't brand me a Luddite just because I can't get excited by on-line retail therapy, the latest supercharged model from Lotus or digital dross.

ON THE TRAIN
Yes, I do bang on about dratted mobile phones. I don't have one. I don't want one.

I scoff at the posing and preening and ludicrous jitterbugging on our streets. I despair at the blaring and bleeping and shameless vocals on our public transport.

I'm an old fogey who knows this whole business will be exposed one day soon as the biggest confidence trick ever to be played on a sophisticated people who simply confused trendy technology with meaningful communication.

Until then, I'll have to suffer in silence and pass on cautionary tales from my occasional trips beyond the county boundaries.

My return train journey from Liverpool Street to Norwich starred a good-looking woman of about 45, bristling with business acumen as she prepared for a mission abroad.

I know her full name, how to spell it, where she lives, her home telephone number, when and where she'll be staying in a Far East hotel and which newspaper and magazine will be delivered to her house when she gets back.

She stopped short of giving her credit card details and bank account number when whoever was on the other end decided they were not essential "at this moment in time".

The woman, sitting adjacent to me, was on her mobile phone for a good hour of the journey. I tried to read a book and ignore her strident voice, but it was impossible to escape all her planning and personal paraphernalia.

Well, my dear, your details are safe with me. I'm not an unscrupulous opportunist looking for a place to burgle or a well-heeled and attractive woman to stalk. But I cannot vouch for everyone else within hearing distance – probably the entire compartment.

Still, there is one redeeming feature of this sad little mobile soap opera. The bulk of our fellow passengers will have missed most of the main pilot as they chased their own banal storylines in "Ringtones – An Everyday Story of Commuting Folk".

LESSON TWENTY
GOLDEN HOURS

We sipped the last of the summer wine around stubbleglint fields and storehouse hedges. Golden days in October ask to be cherished, a beautiful bonus before leaves and temperatures fall.

This year's sunblessed extras will linger long in the memory.

Our unlikely North Norfolk safari began in the twisting lanes behind Bodham.

I blamed the torrid heat for thinking out loud: "There's no celebrity swagger about this village despite being next door to the Beckhams."

That's East and West Beckham, for those unfamiliar with this part of the county. David and Posh might find such rural backwaters a little off the showbiz pace, but the wife and I were happy to tread boldly along the brambled catwalk.

"Squidgy!" she exclaimed. No, not her pet name for a fellow-raider on Mother Nature's autumn larder, but an immediate commentary on the texture of blackberries dangling at the window.

The word took me back to my plasticine-kneading days at infant school, and the mud-pie malarkey which saw me require a bath before breakfast when at the age of three I discovered the joys of dig-and-douse adventures in next door's garden.

"They'll make perfect blackberry jelly," I retorted, feeling it rather impertinent to complain about finding a glut of over-ripe fruit on an October doorstep. She collected hips and haws as well to broaden the homemade menu.

Mellow Monday coasted into Tarrying Tuesday, young pheasants scurrying for cover and pied wagtails showing off acrobatically as we took our picnic to the outskirts of Itteringham.

Ancient trees turned gnarled smiles on two farmers walking in their sugar beet crops.

We ambled on our long but rewarding way round to the familiar avenue at Alby where we relished our first fruit-picking harvest of the season three weeks earlier. Yes, red had turned to black in countless cases – but the plumpest ones remained tantalisingly out of reach.

"Bet they're squidgy" went up the consoling cry.

A small but busy wind turbine stood guard over the children's bookshop sitting incongruously in the midst of this pastoral scene. Wonder if

Hansel and Gretel ever came this way...

It rained heavily the next day as pots steamed, pans bubbled and jars filled with hedgerow goodness.

A warm October glow had transferred to our kitchen from the edge of Norfolk country lanes.

DIFFERENT WORLD

A tendency to take it all for granted may be one of the inevitable by-products of living next door to the sea for two decades.

A daily stroll to promenade and pier still carries a stimulating edge, especially when the wind has bite and the light bathes everything in sight.

There's the contrast between summer bustle and winter space, narrow streets and open sands, trippers chewing chips on the march and fisher-men creaking ashore in shiny oilskins.

Cromer at work and play. Stolid seaside fare, with few surprises and no concessions to current trends hardly counting against it.

So, if I treat Cromer as a faithful old friend, where to look for a dash of exuberance and extra freedom on the edge of what our forefathers called the German Ocean?

Well, I invariably head down the long road to Hunstanton rather than the long road to Yarmouth. Scarcely a contest if you prefer the distant snarl of tide on shingle to the constant hum of a gas terminal for starters.

Mind you, there are a few obstacles to surmount before words from Lilias Rider Haggard, minted over half a century ago, can request anoth-er airing: "Some enchantment lies upon the coast of North Norfolk which leaves it in memory, not just an impression of peculiar beauty, but a series of pictures standing out as vividly as if you had opened a book."

Caravan hordes still rule the Runtons' clifftop scene all year round – their winter presence after a controversial legal ruling loses none of its original sting – while Sheringham shows the sprawling habit does not view Cromer as a last resort.

After that, as trees turn their backs on icy blasts and windmills, and churches vie for the honour of most familiar landmark, Norfolk's heritage coastline trumpets its power and glory. I suspect most locals who love it pay proper homage in the winter months.

We selected Holkham nature reserve for our family post-festive "blow", confident of finding enough fresh air to go round. This is the biggest reserve in England, extending to over 10,000 acres.

Room to roam, to wander and wonder, cantering horses and scampering dogs sharing a giant stage with folk anxious to make some atonement for seasonal excesses. Many will return when the sun is stronger and the winds softer.

We'll join them for a few more hours in a different world that happens to belong to Norfolk. There can be no chance of ever taking that for granted.

GENTLE JAUNTS

A couple of recent gentle jaunts along and around the North Norfolk coast enabled me to usher into play a few of my favourite words – character, cherish, durable, inviting, peaceful and space.

Perhaps they did emerge all the more readily as an unlikely November sun stirred the soul and brought extra appeal and colour to the familiar.

Many a widespread outbreak of festive shopping fever before Bonfire Night and Remembrance Day made me an easy target for symbols of resistance rooted in check-out free aisles.

I confess to plotting a deliberate path towards a revivalist tent on the village green, marvelling at the uncertainty of country days to come. Does that big blaze of berries portend rough weather? A little bird chirped in my ear:

If on the trees the leaves still hold,
The coming winter will be cold.

Well, that's a relief! Bound to stifle all that moaning about not getting winters like we used to. But how many old wives still believe in their oldest tales?

We sauntered a few healthy hedgerows inland to wonder again how Letheringsett keeps its nerve and rural feel despite a constant snake of traffic through its heart. Piles of golden leaves helped me muffle the groans

It's a delightfully long stretch to Langham after leaving the main Holt to Fakenham highway.

Pheasants, pigs and inkpen branches abound as the eye lifts easily from clearly-defined fields to wide open skies.

There's a rare residence on the right. How did Smokers Hole get that name? I've asked many times but received no reasonable answer. Norfolk ignorance can be bad for your health.

Langham, trim and comfortable, seems to wander off rather absent-mindedly towards wartime runways where the only wings now are in the turkey sheds

Cockthorpe Church plays hide-and-seek among the trees in a 'blink-and-you're-through-it' community.

Morston Church stands castle-like on a knoll, a chunky square tower partly rebuilt in red-brick in 1743 providing a marble-cake flavour.

Stiffkey clings to an eternal belief that no amount of vehicles passing through in search of other coastal charms can destroy its inherent good looks or self-sufficiency – a brave stand slightly easier to take as colourful legions of leaves wait for frost, wind and rain to rout them.

I crunched down the path into a village church full of thanksgivings for diversity of character: justice of the peace Nathaniel Bacon; controversial rector Harold Davidson; part-time farmer and full-time writer Henry Williamson.

Their contrasting talents and temperaments brought notoriety to this little corner of North Norfolk.

I stood quietly on the morning of Remembrance Day in their parish waiting for their names to flutter down from the sturdy tree of time.

ANNUAL TREAT

As the sun beat down on a bleached Norfolk countryside I urged the wife to pull in at the edge of a freshly-shorn barley field.

Time for my annual stubble-treading treat, to renew vows with the coronation of the year despite being stripped of most of its majesty by mechanical monsters.

Romantic images keep tugging me back while the corn turns golden and the year turns ripe. And I don't want to number among multitudes who chant "All Is Safely Gathered In" at church or chapel without having set one foot on the harvest scene.

There are plenty of other sensitive souls on the headlands to join in any scything away of the summers. John Stewart Collis, poet among modern ecologists, worked on the land in the 1940s. The power of the combine harvester went against the grain:

"The age-long, centuries-old tradition of harvesting, of gathering up the year's work, is taken away from the labourers. In their place the one big machine. We look across the land for human beings, and we see –one engine. And in its wake bare fields, no ricks met the eye and no work for thatchers or threshers."

There's A G Street, no stranger to Norfolk pastures, drawing comparisons with his native Wiltshire in the 1930s and reminding us how dear old Richard Jeffries had claimed in 1879 that the next generation of country folk would hardly be able to understand the story of Ruth.

Stubble-treading and memory-gleaning may be dismissed as futility rites, but I'll be there again next year to peer through thick clouds of dust to see rabbits congregating in the middle and workers sharing fourses under the hedge.

ON THE EDGE

Family outings this summer have carried an extra layer of meaning as elder son prepares for university life.

We've ambled down familiar paths for "old time's sake", aiming to prove conclusively that nostalgia and home pride are not confined to those who get withdrawal symptoms the other side of Brandon.

I cannot dictate a specific route – the driver has far more right to do that – but there are certain places where I'm guaranteed to be in jovial mood and likely to pay for tea.

A return visit to Oxburgh Hall made us wonder if all that scaffolding could possibly feel at home in a war-like muster of gatehouse, towers and battlements reflected in a moat. The lads got the usual reminder that the village of Oxborough is spelt differently.

Swaffham, kinder to pedestrians since its spruce up, had men working up the church tower on the eve of a big flower festival.

Castle Acre seemed almost ready for autumn as trees trembled in a sudden draught along the main street.

We had to steal a peek at Rougham so I could recall Ephraim Manning singing his heart out at the Methodist Chapel and Roger Angel earning his wings as a member of a powerful village cricket team.

We took the slow route back to Cromer.

An early-evening meal at Wells, overlooking the busy quay and fast-changing skies, proved a tasty prelude to a coastal treat that never loses its gentle magic.

Stiffkey looked so much busier than usual as scarecrow characters lined the twisting street to drum up support for the village fete. A combine ate hungrily into more acres as the sun set red and dramatic.

Mists rolled over marshes. Geese arrowed above. Hedges stirred with bedtime adventures.

Morston, Blakeney, Cley, Salthouse, Kelling, Weybourne...I whispered the register, knowing all were present and prepared to share secrets with trees bending away from the sea.

No need to ask elder son if he'll be glad to come back between lectures for a refresher course along this campus on the edge for students of blessed Norfolk life.

ANNIVERSARY TRAIL

We celebrated our wedding anniversary in the enticing shadows of Ely Cathedral, such a dominating presence over miles and years.

Viewed from distance it is regularly likened to a huge ship riding at anchor in a misty sea, the prefect image, some might muse, of married fortitude in testing waters.

Open skies and wide horizons demand curtain calls for Fenland characters like Hereward the Wake, Oliver Cromwell and Cornelius Vermuyden. We paid due homage to Freedom Fighter, Lord Protector and Drainage King – and then turned a homeward trek into an impromptu magical history tour of our own.

We took a series of diversions from boring main roads, using "well, we must take advantage while we're in these parts" as a reasonable excise for pottering and probing. Sunshine, birdsong and helpful villagers were bonus ingredients.

Maritime legend Captain George Manby called first for attention in Hilgay churchyard. We followed a narrow avenue of trees with an oaken lych gate at each end. A priest about to celebrate mass pointed us to Manby's tombstone before going back inside "to worry God again".

Born in nearby Denver, eccentric and undervalued Manby died in poverty here in 1854. He invented the rocket lifesaving apparatus as well as a chemical fire extinguisher, elastic sheets for use at fires, harpoons for whaling and improved types of lifeboats, howitzers and dredgers.

Manby deserved many more plaudits in life. His gravestone, carved with little reliefs of a mortar, a ship and an anchor, needs a restoration job.

Next stop, West Dereham, much bigger and, in places, far more attractive than expected. This is the birthplace of Hubert Walter, one of the great medieval administrators who returned to found a monastery here while he was Dean of York. Remains can still be traced at the Abbey Farm.

Walter, who died in 1205, became Archbishop of Canterbury under Richard I. Devotion to his monarch also brought the positions of Lord Chief Justice of England, Lord High Chancellor and Governor of the Realm. I feel the village could to more to recognise their famous son.

Wordsmith of note Robert Forby looked after the flock at Fincham in the early 1800s. He died five years before the publication of his Vocabulary of East Anglia, still a constant source of reference and delight for dialect enthusiasts.

Surprisingly, not a word about his efforts in this or any other direction in a leaflet purchased on entry into the imposing St Martin's Church. Perhaps a little Forby tribute could be "tricolated up" to do him justice.

So much to relish in the Church of the Holy Trinity at Stow Bardolph, but time only to meet a woman with a macabre sense of the "Hareafter".

The Hare Chapel was built on to the church by John Hare in 1624 as "a spacious dormitory for the interment of himself and his family." Monuments and memorials abound, none more extraordinary than the wax effigy in a mahogany case up the corner. Sarah Hare asked for such treatment in her will of 1743 and this is the only funerary wax to survive outside Westminster Abbey.

"We can't top this," I said to the wife as Sarah glared at us through the glass.

Home to Cromer and strawberries for tea. Barton Bendish, Beachamwell, Broughton and Bexwell can wait.

APRIL TRUTHS

"April is the cruellest month," wrote the poet T S Eliot in 1922, probably just after some clever-dick reminded him that this name nearly spelt "toilets" backwards.

Palindromic niceties aside, it's not too exacting to find evidence in support of Mr Eliot's misgivings as megaphones of daffodils shout a stirring invitation.

Easter brings the holiday mood to life after a winter of sizing up brochures and their teasing images.

While excursions to faraway places may have to wait a while, there's plenty of flexing and rehearsing in Norfolk as the sun musters power at last.

Some natives, more sensitive than selfish, start to be wary as the tourist bandwagon gets a fresh coast of paint and spots "full of olde worlde charms" where "time stands still" and "quality of life is all" are subjected to the sort of examination that has desecrated other desirable corners.

I've said it before. I'll say it again. If pushing a relatively quiet and unspoilt area into the spotlight with slick salesmanship is effective, too many people respond and so destroy the very attractions they have come to savour.

Such an irony first stuck home in Victorian Norfolk when Poppyland became a magnet for the arty London set as writer Clement Scott gave it the full "paradise" treatment.

It wasn't long before he was wishing he had kept the discovery to himself to prevent it from turning into "Bungalow Land". Wonder what he'd make of today's Celebcorner around the Burnhams, Brancaster and Blakeney...

April also sends out its annual appeal to stiff-muscled enthusiasts trying to hold back the years. So many personal battles to be waged as a new cricket campaign beckons.

A cruel truth can travel in so quickly from the boundary's edge. The paunch, sadly, is too often mightier than the sward.

STRICT MEDICAL

Grey squirrels bounded across the silent but beautiful parkland. A big log fire crackled an invitation to the Victorian mansion where generations have found learning can be fun.

Holt Hall residential and field study centre, only a mile or so from the North Norfolk town but very much its own world of peace and relaxation, provided an idyllic setting as we felt the first pinch of autumn.

We came in search of The Heart of Norfolk at a weekend house party. While we stopped short of claiming it had suffered fatal cardiac arrest, there was refreshing honesty in assessing some of the county's problems.

How easy it could have been to flop into a cosy old armchair and just talk fondly of days dominated by vibrant dialect, community spirit, quiet lanes, bobbies on bikes and delivery men who piled smiles and banter into cardboard boxes.

We might have covered ourselves in sackcloth and ashes befitting remnants of a lost race, an ethnic minority in our own backyard, bucolic leftovers tied together by passion for the past and fear of the future.

I am pleased to report a far more worldly-wise approach, despite a tranquil backcloth so at odds with much of the Norfolk we left behind for a few days.

Of course there was time to glory in our vernacular and the humour which keeps it company. We revelled in enthusiasms for local books and writers still playing key roles in the fight to maintain our precious sense of identity and place.

We gave sincere thanks for the spirit of survival.

The bonus, though, had to be this warts-and-all appraisal of the county – there were representatives from all areas – with questions too many would prefer to push aside.

Two of our party happy to be described as in the full flush of eventide led a lively debate on the growing number of old folks' homes concentrated in coastal towns like Hunstanton and Cromer.

Ass well as strains on medical resources and serious imbalances in terms of age-groups in communities, there is a little matter of trying to treat institutionalised elderly people with the dignity and interest they deserve.

A tour of "shabby Yarmouth" was prompted by a long-time east coast resident who said he hadn't felt the need to visit the Golden Mile in years. That will sound like heresy to councillors and tourist chiefs who bridle at every criticism instead of asking for honest reasons behind it.

Village apathy and vandalism, market-town sprawl and yobbery, city crime and fear – hardly the sort of menu you would associate with weekend guests seated round a roaring fire in a lovely old mansion.

But Norfolk's reputation for dewin' diffrunt brought a few uncomfortable truths home to roost. I felt honoured to be in the chair for this memorable session of squit, wit...and plenty more.

WELLS SAFARI

It was a morning for compromise after heavy rain gave way to cheery sunshine and winds veering between boisterous and belligerent.

Yes, we'd start Christmas shopping with a promise from me not to moan all over a ritual that had to be faced. In return, I could select our destination.

"Wells," I announced. My wife suspected some sinister motive at first – like all-day closing or a personal appearance by Joan Collins at the Co-op – but we had struck a bargain.

Weybourne, Kelling, Salthouse, Cley, Blakeney, Morston, Stiffkey... bright beads on a precious coastal necklace. So familiar but ever-responsive to the lightest touch.

Lilias Rider Haggard's lines from her Norfolk Notebook of 1946 moved in to console as I anticipated the prospect of parting with money simply because we had arrived at a certain part of the year.

"The cry of the redshank and the distant snarl of tide on the shingle. The long line of woods and rounded hills behind – the pewter-grey sea before – this corner of England which once it holds your heart is more lovely than any place on earth. Beautiful with a hint of secrecy which haunts it..."

I reminded myself that she had also written with great tenderness about the joys of Christmas shopping.

There was the inevitable tractor parked just round the corner into Cley as a pointer to more urgent occupations than dreaming, strolling and birdwatching.

We resisted a diversion to pretty little Warham – "it's the fort that counts," I mumbled shamefully – and started a late-morning rush in Wells. Another car parked beside us, paid and displayed. Seagulls squawked and wheeled over a deserted quayside. I braced myself.

Dazzling sunshine made it impossible to see up Staithe Street and mocked this festive expedition like a snowstorm scoffs at the calendar in May.

Two shopkeepers, eager for chat as much as custom, told us they preferred Sheringham on learning we came from Cromer. "More compact and not so cold" they suggested, with playful shudders to emphasise the point.

I wanted to offer something pertinent about Wells not being quite so hot when it comes to television documentaries lifting the lid on life in this part of North Norfolk. But natural tact confined me to latest bulletins from the Crab Wars. I didn't like that recent programme, as a matter of fact, and felt Wells fully deserved the subsequent public apology.

We bought several small presents, mardled and meandered and winced only when knots of teenagers, presumably taking advantage of their school dinner hour, treated us to lewd and loud language from the bottom of the brantub of brainless bravado.

The Cley tractor hadn't moved but the wind had died and the sun had lost its purpose by the time we peered again over moody marshes and admired the umbers and golds of the reeds.

"This almost makes shopping worthwhile," I sighed, although my wife knows some people will always consider it better to travel then to arrive. Perhaps we'll make it to Hunstanton next December.

POETIC REUNION

My Fenland safari had to be a voyage of discovery. For old friend Edward Storey it was a triumphant return of the poetic native.
We met up again in his home town of Whittlesey, near Peterborough, to share a stage built for memories, humour and fund-raising with a family flavour.

Edward travelled by rail from his comparatively new base in North Wales to be reunited with his spiritual heartland. I took the train from Cromer to test out more "foreign parts" at the behest of sensible folk who spend a lot of time in North Norfolk.

Trevor Storey, Edward's youngest brother, still lives in Whittlesey and he and his wife Jan are fervent supporters of the Cystic Fibrosis Trust. Their only grandchild, Adam, suffers from the disease and they came up with the idea of basing a fund-raising event around Edward's homecoming.

We added more than £700 to the coffers, and Edward paid the inevitable price of local fame. He pumped countless hands, pulled names out of nowhere when confronted with yet another "remember me?" and brushed back those elegant grey locks before signing more copies of his verse and prose.

This was no good-natured professional simply going about his job. More a proudly passionate homespun lad delighted to be ploughing familiar furrows in an area that has inspired so much of his writing career.

He recalled Whittlesey as a town balanced precariously between agri-culture and the brick industry. He remembered his father lifting him up to look over the wall of the brickyard kiln where he worked and pointing to distant lights of Peterborough pin-pricking the horizon.

"One day you might go there"... he made it sound like the end of a lifetime's adventure which only a few achieved.

Edward paid tribute to the splendidly-named Miss Speechley, the teacher who introduced him to the joys of Oliver Twist, Tom Sawyer, Treasure Island and other adventures to feed the young imagination.

Another Whittlesey-born author, L P Hartley, wrote: "The past is a foreign country." Edward Storey regularly reminds us that in going back to what's no longer there we can learn:

"Our paths are set
The roots remain unsevered as the stream
in which we swam no-one can now pollute."

He headed back to Discoed, near Presteigne in Powys, where his genial company and uncluttered approach to the arts have already made him a big favourite.

I returned to Norfolk as a hazy heat hung listlessly over the flat earth. Ely Cathedral's dominance of the landscape for miles around came again as an uplifting experience, a huge ship riding at anchor in a calm and oft-times misty sea.

The gateway in and out of my native county begged no poetic lines. Brandon halt, buildings boarded up or falling down, scruffy and forlorn, surrounded by what I wanted to call a bombsite – until I realised that could be unkind to the explosives industry.

Thetford little better, drab and claustrophobic with new houses apparently determined to tumble on to the track. Thankfully, a few compartments of colour and cordiality to come.

A green and white mixture from the bowls club alongside to lift spirits at Attleborough. And a lovely whiff of Brief Encounter at Wymondham.

Much more like it!

CRIES OF RELIEF

Over the bridge of sighs to autumn, season of mists and mellow fruitfulness. Yes, the annual pilgrimage brings just enough silence and space to take stock. Listen very carefully and you must hear those usual cries of relief:

From jaded parents, so pleased to hand back their children to rejuvenated teachers who can't wait for the next round of inspections, tests, changes and insults.

From poor old farmers, barns full to remind them that seedtime and harvest do keep on troshin' despite the best efforts of the Common Agricultural Policy.

From tractor drivers, able to go for a short spin down a country road without attracting every vehicle in Norfolk driven by a Jeremy Clarkson lookalike.

From uplifted vicars excited at the prospect of their largest congregations since Easter and of the chance to tell backsliders there's room for all to be safely gathered in.

From Cromer pedestrians, on the verge of writing to Michael Palin for a few travelling tips after four months of trying to cross the road without having a nervous breakdown.

From seaside traders, who can now stop pretending it's just one great big jolly, juicy jackpot of a jamboree from May until August (those selling chips, ice-cream and beer don't need to pretend.)

From all right-minded natives refusing to feel guilty for simply feeling good about having the old place back to themselves for a precious while.

There are other good reasons for misquoting Robert Browning with "Oh, to be in Norfolk now that autumn's there", most of them connected, quite reasonably with the deification of traditional rural virtues. Quiet walks, glorious colours and home-made blackberry jam top several lists.

Another familiar sound goes with this year's sighs. The rustle of consultation papers from the Countryside Commission, deeply concerned about what's happening to our areas of outstanding natural beauty, ought to signal a winter of serious discontent among all who claim to care.

Sadly, I fear this latest initiative will suffer the same dust-gathering fate as countless other well-meaning documents issued in the name of rural protection during the past two or three decades.

Unprecedented pressure on the Norfolk and Suffolk coastlines from tourism, recreation and erosion demand something far more urgent than a consultation paper and a fond hope that "ideas and energy can be harnessed to keep those areas special for generations to come."

As a recent letter to the *Eastern Daily Press* from Burnham Thorpe underlined, the North Norfolk coastal strip can resemble a massive car park when hordes descend on an "unspoilt" area.

Yet we know those with most influence will spend the winter reciting the tourism gospel rather than reaching out for possible answers to vexed questions.

That is why my customary sigh of relief at the arrival of autumn is coupled with a wail of anxiety. Too many now treat them as areas of outstanding natural booty, maximising commercial advantages at the expense of the environment.

We would do well to spread that truth with the blackberry jam.

WHIFF OF PAST
A whiff of lilac invariably puts me on the scent of childhood. It goes back to those two bushes, one white and the other mauve, standing guard

either side of the old well in our garden.

Colours blotting out blackness below where a crazy swinging pail could play havoc with young muscles and young nerves. Smells floating up to my bedroom on a balmy breeze with a promise of full summer riches to come.

The window opened on my little acre of Norfolk. If you listened carefully as dusk squeezed through the hedges, birds and insects composed an instant lullaby while older boys' yells mocked those already sent up wooden hill to blanket fair.

My burning resentment at being put to bed so early, long before orchard cricket matches had been properly concluded, gave way to an unlikely sense of contentment as I lolled on the window ledge.

Views, smells and sounds joined forces to tell me I was really a lucky lad.

I knew nothing of town or city life in those austere years after the Second World War, but I guessed it couldn't be so good as this.

They didn't have our sort of quiet as the sun went down. Even older boys on my patch surrendered suddenly to the spell.

Isolation begat tranquillity as I counted the number of potatoes, beans, onions and carrots coming through in well-ordered rows.

A beam of fresh light from the lamp in our kitchen below helped my mental arithmetic.

Even when the old well tried to throw an ominous shadow over my pastoral musings, the mood had been set too firmly for village magic to falter.

I've gathered lilacs again this bountiful May, unashamedly catching a whiff of a past where listening, looking, sniffing and feeling came naturally.

CRYSTAL CLEAR

A woman returned home from a psychic fair with a crystal ball. "How much did they sting you for that?" asked her husband.

"£55," she answered, rather sheepishly.

"£55!" exploded her husband. "They must have seen you coming!"

LESSON TWENTY-ONE
INSPIRING FIGURES

I felt the comforting presence of an old master as new pupils filed into the classroom.

Gresham's School at Holt was the setting for my Saturday morning workshops designed to unravel a few mysteries and misconceptions hanging over the Norfolk dialect.

Members of The Society of Teachers of Speech and Drama, in the county for their summer conference, were ready for a good mardle. We had met and mingled informally the night before on a Broads cruise when there were far more questions than harnsers.

The size of my task could be measured by the range of backgrounds represented here in this famous old seat of learning.

A partnership from Sri Lanka nodded greetings.

An English couple who have run a drama school in Kuwait for several years waited for the curtain to rise.

A woman from Preston told me about her recent holiday guide who had billed himself as "Lawrence of Romania". Suddenly, the idea of such a cosmopolitan gathering took on extra appeal.

That old dialect master Dick Bagnall-Oakeley, who taught generations of Gresham's scholars from all over the world, would have relished this sort of get-together.

Dick was asked to hold the fort for a couple of weeks as a geography teacher at Gresham's when he was 25. He accepted – and stayed for the rest of his career. He would often break into his native Norfolk dialect both at the school where he had been a pupil and while delivering natural history lectures throughout the region and beyond.

He died in 1974 but remains a key inspiration in the campaign to promote and preserve our vernacular as a vibrant part of Norfolk life. I'm sure he was tuned in as those delegates, some from faraway places, tried to hunt down the authentic sound. I shared my enthusiasm for home grown delights like the lyrics of The Singing Postman, the Boy John Letters from Sidney Grapes, Bible stories in Norfolk dialect by Colin Riches and John Kett's local verses.

Perhaps the most telling episode in either packed session came with a call for volunteers to read the opening lines of Arnold Wesker's Roots, the play which has put Norfolk on an international stage since 1958.

Wesker set a trend few have seen fit to follow when he made genuine attempts to find out how Norfolk people really talk and also included notes on pronunciation to help "furriners" get somewhere near the accent and intonation.

Predictably, most brave efforts soon floundered in murky Mummerzet waters – but exasperation and deep disappointment among impromptu performers promised renewed zeal in the mission to get it right.

I was assured Norfolk is not alone in being badly misrepresented on television, radio and stage. The best way forward, urged one passionate delegate, is for each abused area to fight its own corner until phoney phonetics dry up.

At least we've got Dick Bagnall-Oakeley on our side.

MEDIA FRIENDS

The past has a habit of beckoning you into reflective corners to sort out wheat from chaff when old friends and colleagues die.

After all, there's a natural tendency to gush forth platitudes and pleasantries in the wake of sad news rather than adopt a more measured and meaningful stance.

I try to make a custom of telling folk what I think of them while they're alive – a dangerous course in some cases – and that can help when it comes to the virtually impossible task of summing up a human existence in a few words or a few minutes.

Thankfully, the recent loss of two old media mates begged no embarrassingly large sacks of chaff as I winnowed through the memories. They knew how much I liked them and admired them in their respective fields.

I was still wet behind the ears as a cub reporter when Bill Coller arrived to put down deep roots in Norfolk with his family.

Evacuated from Dunkirk and later posted to the Middle East, North Africa, Italy and Greece, Bill was just about ready for us in the early 1960s.

We worked together on the Dereham and Fakenham Times, Bill developing Wells as his regular beat in the name of Quaysider while preaching the West Ham football faith to anyone who'd listen. Wiry and chirpy, as befits a former professional boxer, he showed me how to put a punch into the tamest article, leading with a sharp adjective and following up with a surprise simile.

Bill's shrewd advice and cheerful company, coupled with expert guidance from chief reporters Charles Sharp and Don Urry, made my Dereham days more productive and progressive than expected, not least by the top brass in Norwich!

I kept in regular touch with Bill and his family. Daughter Tina rang to tell me he had died at 86.

"He always talked about the good times you shared..."
John Mills died of cancer at 59. He was already an established broadcaster on joining BBC Radio Norfolk at opening time in 1980. It didn't take him long to earn a reputation as the county's most argumentative presenter.

John did enjoy playing devil's advocate on his Sunday morning phone-in show when important local matters were up for discussion, but he could cut through all the bluster and blaring with one incisive comment, one stinging put -down.

He read widely, researching thoroughly and thought carefully about what he was saying on air. That measured approach bought valuable time to probe callers and get more out of them, especially when evasive tactics threatened to smother the issue.

Big glasses gave him an owl-like appearance to go with the undoubted wisdom that characterised his programmes for more than 25 years.

John bore his fatal illness with bravery and dignity, choosing to continue to deal with listeners' problems for as long as possible rather than wallow in his own.

And to those who posed the question so often during my years alongside John on broadcasting duties at Norfolk Tower...yes, he did have a sense of humour.

Just a bit more calculated and subtle than most.

SADLY NEGLECTED

When she died at 92 the *Eastern Daily Press* called Doreen Wallace "a latter-day Boadicea".

As a social campaigner and writer she gained widespread admiration as a key figure in a 40-year campaign to abolish what she described as "the iniquitous tithe tax" on agricultural land.

Born in Cumbria of Scottish parents, she moved to Norfolk to take a teaching post in Diss after the First World War and over the years wrote nearly 50 novels as well as short stories, poems and several works of non-fiction.

Add artist, academic, farmer and mother to her job descriptions and you have some idea of the breadth of this remarkable woman's talents and achievements.

For all that, Doreen Wallace (1897–1989) remains largely neglected by the reading public in an area where she left such a bold mark.

Her books are out of print, like those of so many women writers, and we wait for an overdue reawakening of interest in a highly-aware social commentator, a chronicler of life in country towns and villages, not unlike Mrs Gaskell of the northern communities.

Sir John Betjeman was an ardent admirer: "Her books are all her own and I like them very much," he said.

Perhaps it will take a similar song of praise from a current literary lion to roar life into a revival campaign.

In the meantime, commendable local efforts are coming from enthusiastic supporters of the Wallace cause, including book-loving pair Helen and Bill Kennett of Harleston.

They have brought out a facsimile copy of *Days and the Years*, poems by Doreen Wallace originally published in 1951 by Giles Dixey.

June Shepherd, who wrote Wallace's biography five years ago but had to rely on an American publisher, provided a copy of this scarce volume of verses and also penned the preface.

It was as a poet that Doreen Wallace was first published between 1917 and 1919 while a student at Somerville College, Oxford. Dorothy Sayers, who became such a stylish writer of detective stories, was one of her contemporaries.

Days and the Years breathes of wistful longing, lost opportunities, unrequited love and deep affection for the countryside and natural world. Some of the verses carry too much hurt for comfort.

I did my little bit to nudge this outstanding character back into the spotlight she deserved by including her in my book Norfolk Heroes a few years back.

Perhaps this collection of "gentle, gossamer" verses will herald a big push out of the shadows for a major writer and campaigner.

MUSIC'S BALM

It had been a tough day, notwithstanding juicy temptation on the annual bop-along strawberry rows.

"Punnet" said the wife as we scanned the crop at Antingham.

"OK," I replied, "Next year we'll go picking at Decingham."

With that dreadful salute to popular culture behind us, nature exacted swift revenge as my back, knees, thighs and other less-than-supple departments cried out for weigh-in time.

I sought sweet consolation in prospect of Sunday fireside teas in winter blessed with strawberry jam.

Easing into my favourite chair in the study, I tuned into the sound of summer as England and Australia clashed in one-day cricket combat.

Bad light stopped play outside. Bad back held up work inside. I needed physical and spiritual resuscitation. A good walk and soothing music were in order.

How lucky that Cromer could provide both.

Gordon Dodson is one of those talented neighbours for whom a chance meeting invariably turns into a lengthy mardle. His measured views, love of words and cheerful countenance make him a marked man on daily rounds.

He read law at Cambridge and was a barrister before being ordained.

Now retired to the North Norfolk coast, he is Canon Emeritus of Norwich Cathedral, assistant organist at Cromer parish church and in constant demand to entertain at the piano.

It was while he was vicar at Snettisham that Gordon met Bryan Ellum, a renowned church organist who had performed widely both as soloist and as accompanist.

The Dodson-Ellum partnership has blossomed over 30 years and here they were when I needed them most to present an evening programme for the benefit of struggling strawberry pickers and anyone else requiring melodic balm.

Cromer's wonderful church dedicated to Ss Peter and Paul in the centre of town stages summer concerts and recitals through to the end of September. Better judges than me suggest this well be ticked off as one of the most refreshing Tuesday tonics.

Bryan, a church organist since the age of 13, encouraged us to sit up straight with Samuel Sebastian Wesley's stirring Choral Song and Fugue. His father Samuel Wesley was dubbed the English Mozart, and it soon became apparent why as his Sonata in G featured in the first piano duet. It only came to light a couple of years ago.

Alfred Hollins (1865 – 1942) was blind from birth but a marvellous ear for music produced items such as Intermezzo in D Flat.

After Bryan's telling tribute on this score, he again teamed up with Gordon on piano for Three Legends by Dvorak, full of surprising diversions as well as being lush and romantic.

"We've saved the best wine till last" said our esteemed entertainers before pouring their talents on piano and organ into Variations on an Original Theme by Ben Burrows.

Gordon Dodson's new grandson Zebedee, just over three weeks old, behaved impeccably in a pew at the back.

"He was awake for part of the time as well," beamed a proud granddad.

"So was I!" exclaimed a grateful neighbour with a taste for strawberries and the cream of local musicians.

AUTHENTIC VOICE

What a glorious autumn double! Gripping Norfolk yarns on a national stage – with a truly authentic Norfolk voice to present them.

I refer to stories carved out of rural misery a century ago by Mary

Mann, a sadly-neglected writer, broadcast every afternoon last week on BBC Radio 4. They were brought to vibrant life by actress Patience Tomlinson, her proud Norfolk roots helping to silence that accursed chorus of Mummerzet voices holding sway so often when it comes to our distinctive accent.

Patience – and the irony in the name won't be lost on those who have long campaigned for an end to gross misrepresentation – was born at Brancaster, where her father, Robert, was rector.

The family moved on to Wolferton and Docking, and Patience attended St Michael's School at Ingoldisthorpe before heading for boarding school in Clacton.

For a year between school and the start of drama studies she worked in the public library at King's Lynn. Her first professional acting job was in The Matchmaker at Ipswich, in the old theatre in Tower Street, and she also savoured a coupled of seasons on stage at Southwold – "paid summer holiday, really."

Patience's father retired to Stanhoe. He died in 1993 but her mother still lives in the village.

"I get back there as often as I can with my family, and it will always be home," Patience told me. She is married to an actor, Jeffrey Perry, and they have a daughter, Eleanor, who also relishes every chance to "escape" to Norfolk.

Patience, with an extensive career in the theatre and more than 1500 broadcasts to her credit, was a natural choice to read Mary Mann's harrowing tales of Victorian Norfolk. She can do most accents and dialects, and shares deep concern at the way all branches of the national media regularly mock her native tongue.

"They wouldn't dare confuse Lancashire and Yorkshire, and yet poor old Norfolk has suffered dreadful abuse. Let's hope this series heralds the start of a more enlightened era," she said.

An ardent admirer of Mary Mann's work, Patience would love the chance to go "on the road" with a presentation of the kind of stories she has just read on the wireless. A Norfolk tour to include the village of Shropham, where the writer settled on marrying in 1871 and which served as the setting for her celebrated Fields of Dulditch stories, would provide a fitting showcase for the talents of two outstanding local mawthers.

DEFENDING LUCILLA

I carried a bit of Breckland into the heart of London on a day of brooding skies and stifling heat.

My excuse for capital punishment centred on the reputation of a

Norfolk woman who took on unforgiving soil and uncompromising military might in the Stanford Battle Area.

My mission was to speak up for Lucilla Reeve as the award-winning BBC Radio 4 documentary department prepares a programme about the Breckland villages that vanished when the Army requisitioned the land in 1942 and never returned it as promised.

Lucilla, illegitimate daughter of a parlour maid, rose to become land agent at the Merton estate. Like many at the time, she flirted with Oswald Mosley's Blackshirt movement before taking on one of the estate farms and creating order out of chaos.

When the military moved in, she refused to move out. She continued to live in her house at Bagmore Farm until the sight of tanks churning up her fields and knocking down her barns proved too much.

Lucilla acquired wooden chicken huts for her new abode and set them just outside the northern boundary of the battle area.

Defiant Miss Reeve waited for the chance to go home. It never came. As years passed, the physical and mental strains took their toll and she hanged herself from a beam in one of the sheds on October 30, 1950.

She remains a truly enigmatic figure at the core of this compelling Norfolk episode, a stubborn woman who turned into a refugee on her own land. A thorn in the military establishment's side, she posed awkward questions still worth asking today.

Who promised that the five annexed villages would be returned to their inhabitants? Why were those promises never honoured? How close did Lucilla come to accepting a plan to leave the area altogether?

Other intriguing questions about Miss Reeve also stay unanswered. Who was her father? Who paid for her private education in London? What did other locals really think of her?

There are clues. Her diaries, letters and private papers haven't survived, but she penned numerous articles for the *Eastern Daily Press* and Farmers' Weekly. They were collected together in her books, *The Earth No Longer Bare*, *Farming On A Battle Ground* and *The Pheasants Had No Tails*.

I read extracts, including some of her plaintive verses, to help paint a picture of a doughty Norfolk fighter.

I happened across a first edition of W G Clarke's *In Breckland Wilds* on the eve of my visit to Broadcasting House in London. Published in 1925 and written by the naturalist who gave the area its name, it is still a stunning read.

PERFECT TIMING
So where were you when the Great Heatwave ended with a spectacular show of heavenly fireworks in the summer of 2006?

My eerie experience last Wednesday evening prompts that question in certain knowledge I'll have few rivals in the "rum ole dew!" stakes.

Thankfully I can produce dozens of reliable witnesses to back a story of pyrotechnics and a remarkable coincidence at the Strangers' Club on Elm Hill in Norwich.

After a splendid supper and torrents of informal mardling, I was invited to share favourite Norfolk yarns, readings and reflections in the upper room of this building at the heart of the city's priceless heritage. Members and guests gave thanks for open windows and we peered down on cobbled history. I wandered slowly along memory lane so as not to stumble too often in sticky going.

Then I sought a spot of shade under at traditional hedgerow with dialect hero Sidney Grapes, selecting one of his Boy John Letters to underline their evergreen qualities.

My choice fell on A Wet Summer, first published in the *Eastern Daily Press* in August, 1954, an epistle bemoaning the effects of too much soggy weather on the local farming picture.

"We shull be a'pullen a tha' beet a tha' mornen, an arter the corn in tha arternoon, wen tha' dew is orf...That rained on St.Swiffen's, so wot ken yer expect." Suddenly, just as we were chuckling at these refreshing memories of "good old days" when rain paid regular calls, humour and humidity gave way to an ear-splitting, eye-dazzling farewell concerto for our lengthy dry spell.

Thunder, lightning and lashing rain nearly tempted me into a line about "the wrath of Grapes" but I satisfied myself with admiring glances and meaningful nods at picking out such perfectly appropriate material.

I have delivered the Norfolk gospel against stormy backcloths before – sessions at Weston Longville, Hingham, Northrepps, Thornham and Neatishead spring to mind – but this has to be the best supporting act with sound effects in a long and extinguished career. In fact, I got so carried away with the uncanny flavour of it all that I overlooked the obvious postscript to this dramatic soiree with friendly Strangers.

The Boy John Letters invariably ended with the latest philosophical gem from Aunt Agatha. To impress my audience even more I should have rushed to an offering from August, 1949:

"PS Aunt Agatha hearnt got northin to say, cos she's a coverin' up the lookin glasses an' a putting the nives away cos there's a thunderstorm a cumin."

HARD MAN RON
I cannot recall an event so dominated by someone not there. Talk about a spectre at the feast...

The old boys' reunion at Carrow Road, marking the 30th anniversary of Norwich City's elevation to soccer's top flight for the first time, went ahead without headmaster Ron Saunders.

Perhaps that ought to be "taskmaster" as stories flowed about his muscle-numbing training routines up and down the slopes of Mousehold. His charges still wince at the memory, pain hardly eased by grudging acceptance that it fashioned enough stamina to stay the promotion course.

Not quite "well, six of the best never did me any harm" at the school get-together for former pupils in February, 2002. More like "I suppose the ends justified the means" from the escape committee on returning to the site of the tunnel they dug three decades earlier.

We were given an intriguing insight into the Saunders "hard man" psychology by Terry Allcock, on the Canary coaching staff at the time. Physiotherapist Jeff Granger hinted there were more injuries from training than from matches themselves, and he didn't have today's ultra-sophisticated equipment to treat them.

Players who exceeded all expectations in that 1971-72 campaign recounted horror stories that may have grown extra horns with passing seasons. Old press reporters, myself and colleague Bruce Robinson, could not exaggerate the amount of caution and tact needed to deal with such a single-minded manager.

Through it all, however, trumpeted the clear message – Ron Saunders' achievements speak for themselves.

He took the club to the top division for the first time, despite meagre resources and widespread doubts. He followed that epic journey by masterminding City's first appearance in a Wembley final.

When his "sorry not to be with you" letter was read out at the recent celebration dinner, I half expected it to be accompanied by a chorus of "I did it my way".

Other talking points of that memorable weekend include Kenny Foggo's refusal to grow old like the rest of us – several jealous colleagues claimed he had to be on youth pills – and Duncan Forbes' "green" approach to humour...

His shameless recycling of old jokes was worth a yellow card at least, especially when it came at the expense of fellow-defender Dave Stringer. Still, a certain manager did insist on making the most of thin material.

I must add a personal postscript to all tributes duly paid to Duncan Forbes on his departure from Carrow Road after 33 years of unstinting service on and off the pitch.

Throughout my seasons as a Canary scribe, most of them in the 1970s, he never once quibbled over anything written about him, not even references to "raw meat", "more bookings than Fred Pontin" and "Ron Saunders' standard bearer on the field."

He did start unfounded rumours about David Stringer peeling oranges in his pocket to avoid handing them round on the bus to Blackburn, He did ask me quietly (I went deaf in just one ear for 25 minutes) if "ebullient" really meant he had a chance of playing for Scotland.

I gave him that label after a typically wholehearted display in the face of a relentless red tide at Anfield. Duncan was by no means the most talented player on parade – but he was the bravest by far. Liverpool fans saluted his unvarnished efforts with genuine warmth.

When we played cricket together in charity matches at Beetley a few years later, Duncan proved old habits die hard by chastising the "referee" for failing to uphold an lbw appeal. Mind you, that shout could be heard at Gressenhall, Longham, North Elmham, Hoe and Swanton Morley...so there was a fair chance of at least one vote in his favour.

An outstanding personality who made the most of his strengths but never sulked about his flaws.

FEISTY BUT FUN

Phyllis Ellis, redoubtable Queen of Wheatfen Broad, taught me all I should have known about public service broadcasting.

She brought her own specialised agenda for regular appearances on BBC Radio Norfolk's Dinnertime Show, lambasting bodies and organisations which had fallen short of her high standards, particularly when it came to conservation and teaching.

I dubbed her "Miss Marple With Claws".

She took that as a compliment, suggesting I would now do better to pay attention rather than interrupt. At least I got my homework in on time.

The retired schoolmistress and widow of people's naturalist Ted Ellis spoke her mind and left scant room for disagreement.

But she had a wicked chuckle and a ready smile for those brave enough to try.

Feisty, but fun, Phyllis, who died in 2004 at 90, made me laugh, listen and look again at our Norfolk as she read one of her beloved Ted's perfectly-formed essays.

Perhaps the rest was just her way of getting attention, clearing the decks for a simple act of worship that stretched the Ellis crusade into another era.

BROTHERS TO FORE

It may be a bit dodgy to hail something as unique or worthy of a place in the record books

However, I am confident that a proud family hat-trick puts my former grammar school in Swaffham top of the mardling class.

Retired Methodist minister Andrew MacKenzie gave the after-lunch speech at the 2004 reunion of the Old Hamondians' Association at the George Hotel.

He was following in familiar footsteps...Brother John did the honours with style the year before. Brother Don started this remarkable sequence the year before that with memorable batch of anecdotes.

Old Hamondians' secretary Ted Heath remarked: "I can't believe this sort of family treble has eve happened before, and they each responded so eagerly to the call."

Andrew attended Hamond's from 1948 until 1953. He left to join the RAF as a boy apprentice, but later settled for a dramatic change in career as he trained for the Methodist ministry and went to Kenya as a missionary for 12 years. He returned home to take up posts in Derbyshire and Scotland before retirement.

Don and John went into teaching, both becoming headmasters. Don, at Hamond's 1952 – 1959, completed his classroom career at Buxton, near Alysham, while his younger brother – one of my contemporaries at grammar school between 1955 and 1962 – was a headmaster in Kent.

The MacKenzie boys arrived in Norfolk in 1946 with parents Frank and Charlotte, and settled in Sporle just three miles from Swaffham.

I recall Frank MacKenzie as a popular local Methodist preacher taking our Sunday school anniversary services at Beeston Chapel in the 1950s.

As my house captain at Hamond's, leading the fight for the Bell cause (yellow) against Wilson (green), Drury (blue) and Lee Warner (red), John MacKenzie showed exceptional faith in my meagre sporting talents.

He once selected me for a football match because (a) there we no one else available; (b) to throw our opponents' marking system into disarray; and (c) to hit them on the break while I made them laugh.

We lost by quite a few.

We did share a brave last-wicket stand in a house cricket match against Wilson, nearly doubling the score before he ran me out. We came second by quite a margin. Still, the MacKenzie mardlers can now celebrate on outstanding hat-trick on the old boys' podium. They deserve bonus points for holding the attention of one of the most notoriously difficult audiences in the business.

SIDEWAYS STANCE

Too long a prophet without proper honour on his own midden, Sid Kipper is at last attracting deserved rations of adoration.

The self-styled Norfolk megastar combines writing, singing and story-telling in such seamless fashion it is difficult to know where to fit him on the entertainment menu.

Perhaps "talented all-rounder with sideways stance" offers the most useful clue, as Sid continues to ask fresh followers where they've been this past decade or so.

Performances on stage and in print mark him as our leading cultural ambassador, failing lamentably to live up to his own maxim that a pleasure shared is a pleasure halved.

His literary opus, Cod Pieces (in crispy banter), filleted to perfection with the help of alter ego Chris Sugden, can only enhance a growing reputation for top-class "squilture".

Yes, it is necessary to invent a new word to describe this potent mixture of squit and culture. Sid takes it all over the country, and occasionally abroad, to show Norfolk is way ahead of the field in lateral thinking.

Cod Pieces is a tasty collection of short stories and tall tales from the small village of St Just-near-Trunch. Sid will be touring nationally next spring with the show of the same name, no doubt explaining exactly where the village can be found.

Several classic yarns get a glossy new coast of effulgence, including David Kipperfield, The Pied Blowpiper of King's Lynn, Sleeping Beauty and the Beast, Three Gruff Billy Goats and My Bootiful Mawther. (Yes, you've got it, you've really, really got it!)

Peter Pain is a modern fable about a man in North Walsham who refuses to grow up. Bunfight at the OK Chorale is set in the old Tame East. Bigots Against Tolerance is the startling manifesto of Farmer Trout's extreme right-wing political party.

Dot Kipper's Handy Household Hints, including how to make an anti-macasserole, the local vicar's Letters to the Truncheons and How the Coypu Dug Its Grave (from the St Just So stories by Rudyard Kipper) call out cheerfully for attention.

My favourite, however, has to be the shamefully unsporting episode of 1931 when St Just faced their old cricket rivals, Burningham, in the final of the North Norfolk Tea Service.

The Burningham Bodyline saga will make your Wisden teeth wobble.

FAMILY ROLE

A Norfolk woman played a key role in putting the county on an international stage.

Hilda Bicker and her family lived at Beck Farm at Redenhall, the setting for Arnold Wesker's Roots, second of his celebrated autobiographical trilogy of plays.

Wesker readily acknowledges that the Bicker family provided the background and inspiration for Roots. Mrs Bryant is the obvious reincarnation of Hilda Bicker – the playwright's mother-in-law.

It was in January, 1957 that Wesker went to stay with his wife's parents at Beck Farm. Dusty Bicker had been brought up there and she inspired the central character of Beatie Bryant in Roots, a play dealing with problems of communicating thoughts and feelings.

Wesker emphasised his Norfolk setting with dialogue written in the local dialect, a move destined to draw so much criticism over the years about actors failing to get it right.

I recall him getting in touch with me just before a BBC television "revival" of Roots to apologise in advance for liberal use of "Mummerzet" tones in the production. His fears were well founded.

For a play concerned so much with the power of language, speech patterns and silences are essential to the overall theme.

In his introduction to the play first presented at the Belgrade Theatre, Coventry, in May, 1959, with Joan Plowright in the main role, Wesker says: "This is a play about Norfolk people; it could be a play about any country people and the moral could certainly extend to the metropolis.

"But as it is about Norfolk people it is important that some attempt is made to find out how they talk. A very definite accent and intonation exists and personal experience suggests that this is not difficult to know."

He then offers a guide to pronunciation, a guide clearly left in the wings many times since.

Roots is hardly a flattering picture of Norfolk life, although there is plenty of humour, especially in the hands of old horseman Stan Mann. Mrs Bryant lives largely on gossip, mundane and predictable.

Wesker gave Hilda Bicker a signed copy of the play. She left it out for visitors to see, although the author doubted she ever read it.
She died at 89 in 1999.

UNFLAPPABLE MRS P

I blame a succession of excellent landladies for my noted lack of sparkle on the domestic front.

In between leaving home in 1962 and getting married just over a couple of decades later, I threw myself on the mercy of Norfolk mother-figures for whom a world-shy waif represented just one more little chore on their daily rounds.

Longest serving – no, make that longest suffering – among them was Pauline Preece, the legendary and much-loved Mrs P, who took me under her unflappable wing next door to what was then the county cricket ground at Lakenham.

Mrs P died just a few days short of her 83rd birthday. When I last saw her in a nursing home, she laughed at the suggestion I had come to pay rent still owed and to apologise yet again for upsetting the budgie and other members of her little menagerie.

Loose gossip still surrounds a certain incident over 30 years back when a rare sense of adventure took me into Mrs P's kitchen while she was out at work. Beans on toast, without burning either, represented a major breakthrough...but in my triumph I forgot to switch off the gas after huffing out the flames.

My oversight featured prominently in a distraught telephone call to the newspaper office some hours later. Mrs P's dogs, Pepi and Bruce, had watery eyes and nasty tizzicks in the throat. Mrs P's cat, Timmy, had watery eyes and a pronounced cough. Mrs P's budgie, Colin, had fallen off his perch.

Mrs P, providentially, did not light up her customary cigarette on arriving home. She gave up smoking soon after. I like to think I played a small part in helping her to kick the habit.

Renowned for her charitable instincts, she exonerated me from all malicious intent but imposed a lifetime ban on me entering her kitchen again on my own. Colin recovered sufficiently to lead a chorus of support.

Other escapades during my days at Geoffrey Road included hiding in her wardrobe and leaping out to claim I was her bank manager – based loosely on a popular TV advert of the time – and dancing round her bed at 5am when England's cricketers recaptured the Ashes in Australia in February, 1971.

She got up and made a pot of celebratory tea.

Mrs P exacted a measure of revenge through her notorious inability to remember names. We sat up way past midnight as she tried to pin down an actress with a throaty voice. All my suggestions simply met with more exasperation.

We decided to resume the great guessing game on the morrow. I'd just dropped off when Mrs P banged on my bedroom door and yelled "Glynis Johns!"

Goodness knows what the neighbours thought of that.

Mrs P's charitable work extended to newspaper colleagues who needed a "safe house" in which to sort themselves out after a spot of overindulgence. Her mixture of black coffee and maternal sympathy forestalled many a late-night drama.

She knew sadness and hardship, raising two young children on her own after a tragic road accident left her a widow, but won countless admirers with a cheerful determination that continued throughout her final illness.

She humoured and cared for me expertly throughout the 1i970s, a period of my life when a homely anchor was vital to keep my sense of purpose float.

Perhaps the best tribute I can pay Mrs P is to recall an episode from early days of my broadcasting career. We were encouraged to have one "special character" in mind as we mardled over the microphone.

I settled on a softly-spoken woman surrounded by pets, sipping tea and trying to remember that actor who married the girl who had a sister in Crossroads.

FITCH IN TIME

We owe much to men of the cloth for preaching a true Norfolk gospel over the years. Just before a Victorian age soaked in prettified village scenes bearing no relation to harsh rural life, a country parson compiled what is still regarded as the "bible" for local dialect lovers.

The Rev Robert Forby wrote A Vocabulary of East Anglia, published in 1830, five years after his death. His "Icenian Glossary" took shape while he was rector of Fincham. He had also held livings at Horningtoft, Barton Bendish and Wereham.

Pointing to popular dialects in his introduction, Forby lamented: "Will they not be overwhelmed and borne down by the general onset of the various plans and unwearied exertions for the education of us all?"

Another Norfolk parson made his distinctive mark in 1862 by translating The Song of Solomon into Norfolk dialect. It was printed with translations for 23 other counties at the expense of Prince Louis Bonaparte, in exile in Britain.

The Rev Edward Gillett, then Vicar of Runham, admitted he was not acquainted with a suitable phonetic spelling with which to indicate the "Norfolk drant", but his rendering shows a relatively successful attempt at a reproduction of the dialect. His Song o'Sorlomun was reprinted in 1993 by the Larks Press.

In the 1970s Methodist minister Colin Riches produced two delightful volumes of Bible stories in the local dialect, Dew Yew Lissen Hare and Orl Bewtiful an' New. Several were originally featured on Anglia Television's late-night religious slot.

Now it is time, methinks, to add another name to this distinguished company – the Rev Charles Harold Fitch, Rector of Sheringham in the years before the Second World War.

He wrote and spoke entertainingly in defence of Norfolk language and character, bur rarely gets a mention when members of the "home guard" look towards the survival pulpit.

One of his articles, demanding to be read as I flicked through some old magazines, trumpeted: "There is a reason for everything, even for the Norfolk language. We must never think that a dialect is spoken just by some unaccountable whim of those who use it. Our tongue expresses most graphically our character, and also the conditions, racial, geographical, historical, which go to make it and in which we and our forebears have been living throughout the centuries."

Rousing sentiments from about 80 years ago, but still pertinent today in the fight against dull uniformity.

My favourite stories from the Fitch file concern reaction to the 1931 earthquake. A Norfolk labourer, asked if he felt it, scornfully replied: "No, that I dint. I sleep at the back o' the house."

An old lady told of her experiences: "That wuz terrible, that wuz. Th'ole house began ter rock an' shake an' th'ole bed along wi'it. My ole man he got up an' look out o' the winder, an' I call out, 'John,' I say 'I believer thass th'end o' the wald he' come!' 'Yes, Martha,' he say, 'I believe that hev...no, thass all right. Them shallots is still there!"

FIRST-CLASS TRIBUTE

I was yielding to that obvious temptation to draw close comparisons between much-loved entertainers for whom the label "vulnerable" might have been printed.

George Best, most tantalising footballer of the age, had died a few hours earlier.

Now, on a wet and windy night, it was time for a coastal pilgrimage to remember Norfolk's least likely pop star.

The county's first official salute to Allan Smethurst, the Singing Postman, arrived nearly five years after his death – a period of quiet reflection well in keeping with his soft, melancholy nature.

He would have chuckled at the idea of sharing a dugout with the twinkle-toed genius from Belfast. I heard strains of "Thass a Lot o'Squit" as we put down anchor in the new Harbour Room at Blakeney's British Legion headquarters.

Wiveton fisherman Gary Mears, thrilled by the turnout of about 100 despite driving wind and rain, emphasised the need to pay proper tribute to the man whose winsome and witty comparisons stand as potent signposts to a cherished past.

By the end of an evening when most of his songs had received an enthusiastic airing it was a formality to declare this the launch of Norfolk's Singing Postman Appreciation Society.

"See you next November!" carried genuine relish.

Gary and friends who make up the Old Wild Rovers warmed the gathering with shanties before the Smethurst songbook took centre stage with sets from Winston (the Singing Farmer), Jon Lowe (Suffolk's Singing Postman), his brother Richard Lowe, who works for the National Trust at Brancaster, and Cromer's Danny Platton.

Jon has been at the heart of Suffolk celebrations over the past few years, but revels in strong Norfolk ties. "I had the misfortune to be born in Ipswich but green and yellow blood flows through these veins!" he laughed.

Perhaps a few more of his fellow-enthusiasts over the border will hit the road to Blakeney next year.

Diane Chambers and her husband travelled from Horwich, a suburb of Bolton, to represent Allan's family connections in Lancashire. Des Barney mooched along from Sheringham to share memories of how schoolboy Smethurst first caught the singing and writing bugs.

The whole event jogged along amiably with the minimum of fuss, old friends mardling and singing in the kind of homely pub atmosphere the Singing Postman took as his natural backcloth.

TRANQUIL WATERS

I have often wondered what Broadland pioneers of the 1880s would make of today's bustling holiday scene and expensive projects designed to make it inviting for future generations.

Men like John Loynes, who laid the foundations of the boat-hire industry, and George Christopher Davies, who first brought the area to public attention through his writing. The first edition of Davies' *Handbook to the Rivers and Broads of Norfolk and Suffolk* in 1882 featured John Loynes as the only boatbuilder to advertise.

Less than a decade later, no fewer than 37 builders and owners were listed as having boats for hire. Davies noted: "Each year the tourist stream increases, but, happily there is still plenty of room."

Guide books to the Broads were less than oar-inspiring according to one anonymous reviewer presented with a batch of them to peruse on behalf of the *Nature Magazine* in 1897: "The bulk of the articles are of the feeblest sort by people who, having spent a few days on the Broads, returned to their distant homes imbued with the erroneous impression that they are qualified to enlighten the world with regard to the features and peculiarities of a tract of country difficult of access and still more difficult to appreciate, and the very name of whose towns and villages they had not learned to spell correctly."

The malady lingers on, and as only an occasional visitor to the heart of Broadland, especially in summer, I must be wary of sweeping assertions a century later.

A Saturday afternoon family voyage up the Ant to Barton Broad in a friend's boat, Hunsett Mill demanding a few more clicks of the camera, starred just-arrived crews on hired motor cruisers.

Flashy caps, tentative grips and sheepish wavers gave the holiday game away in some cases, but experienced locals remained cheerful and polite in making allowances. A similar spirit would not go amiss on our packed roads.

FLAMING CHEEK

Iris Tillett, who died in 1997 in Scotland, was appointed county secretary when the Women's Land Army was set up in Norfolk just before the last war.

She recalled her experiences in a book, *The Cinderella Army*, published in 1988, and also on regular visits back to her home county. I enjoyed several mardles with the woman who claimed nothing could surprise her after experiences among the girls in green jerseys.

My favourite snippet from the "red tape" file followed the burning down of the uniform department.

"To our sorrow, a brand new typewriter went up in smoke. When we indented for a new one, they wanted the remains of the old one returned as proof that it was now useless" said Iris. "I refused on the grounds the building had been declared unsafe, and I was not going to allow a member of my staff to risk her life by going in."

Iris got her replacement.

Then there was the hostel landgirl who said she couldn't sleep unless she had a fish and chip summer. Clearly, this could not be supplied in the hostel and so she cycled most evenings to the nearest chip shop four miles away.

It was later discovered her parents had kept a chip shop.

Panic reigned when a mouse landed on a girl's plate as she poured from the hostel gravy jug. A cat chased it across the kitchen. The mouse came to a warm and sticky end as it dived into the jug.

LESSON TWENTY-TWO
CRYSTAL BALL

"Norfolk's patience, tolerance, proud sense of individuality and decidedly dry sense of humour will be sorely tested in the next few years."

That pert little summary could well have been regulation issue for county defenders great and small over the centuries. For someone of my age and disposition, who just missed road-building Romans, urn-burying Saxons, sword-brandishing Vikings and gum-chewing Americans, it carries a particularly potent edge so early in a new millennium.

Some would urge us to be flattered by so much interest in this part of the world where "quality of life" and "time to relax" are more than neat slogans. They claim there's plenty of room to cope with more houses, more residents, more jobs, more traffic, more benefits and more attractions to keep more tourists amused.

Inevitably, there will be more changes, several brought about by pressures dressed up as promises, and I know those clamouring for Norfolk to get in stride behind the rest will shout the loudest. IFor all that, traditional virtues must refuse to budge in some quarters when the wheels of so-called progress turn the fastest.

When the future does throw out a warm hand to grasp old and new together, tactfully and tastefully, then even the most cussed of natives can find a tremor of anticipation to replace the more familiar shudder of trepidation.

Automatic aversion to change is yesterday's habit – unless it looks like the only reasonable answer to yet another direct threat to tomorrow's world.

The true Norfolk-lover will continue to make comparisons beyond the scope of too many who make decisions, and will be proud to be called an old stick-in-the-mud for doing so.

The true Norfolk-lover will eschew passing fads and fashions and hold close those customs and characteristics which give his home a durable reputation for being different.

The true Norfolk-lover will carry on smiling when the old-fashioned roof seems to be on the verge of caving in. A sense of humour weans a sense of proportion and provides useful shelter when the roof does fall in.

Perhaps it is the clearest symptom of approaching old age to spend more time looking back than straining forward. That and using stories way past their tell-by date are the main giveaways. But some comfort can be derived from the old Norfolk saw:" If yew know where yew hev bin, that dunt matter ser much where yew myte be a'gorn, thow that allus pay ter know where yew are."

T S Eliot put it nearly as well when he mused:

Time present and time past
Are both perhaps present in time future
And time future contained in time past.

It is wishing time away that should give most cause for worry as we are teased into trying to see into Norfolk's future. We do it all the while, often confusing it with anticipation and always assuming it will be better over the next hedgerow.

How can we ensure survival rations of respect for past and present? The Norfolk Society for Timeless Enjoyment does carry an appealing ring.

I doubt if real pleasure can be organised. Certainly, you cannot legislate for the whim of the Norfolk soul as it seeks constancy in a fast-changing world. We have our favourite haunts where it is possible to shun the pressure of time, to throw off the yoke of keeping up appearances – and simply keep up.

Long before I moved there to live, I went to Cromer and the North Norfolk coast to remind myself of the glorious things of life. It still works best in winter. An initial nod towards lifeboatman Henry Blogg as he peers out over the North Sea in all weathers. His bronze head and so'wester epitomise the sort of permanence and dependability we crave from our best friends in favourite places.

Clifftop walks at Cromer offer reassurance that time and change need not be inseparable partners. The view back towards town has altered little in a century and gives the impression of being able to stay there as look as you want to look fondly upon it. Tall Regency houses, the mid-Victorian fantasy of the Hotel de Paris and, above them all, the 160-foot tower of the parish church. The old town climbs the cliff to nurture a smile for all seasons.

More receptive visitors give the seal of the day as I turn for home after another refresher course above the waves. Another salute for Blogg as clouds chase each other across the sort of restless sky he must have seen in his dreams.

He was a modest hero, the most reticent of men. Perhaps one of the most telling things he ever said was one sentence of rebuke to a gushing woman visitor who saw him on the promenade and commanded an audience.

A summer storm was driving great breakers up the beach as the woman exclaimed: "Oh, Mr Blogg, isn't the sea beautiful!"

"No, my dear" said old Blogg. "That ent bewtiful. Thass cruel."

As cruel as time has been to less fortunate neighbours along the coast where the breakers of commercialism have rolled over too many homely sands.

It may be out of keeping with these helter-skelter times to laud a spot holding on so doggedly to the past, but I reckon locals and visitors   alike will maintain their vigil to keep Cromer off the trendy map.

You can take the defiant stand inland. A country lane. The corner of a small wood where rooks argue and bluebells put down a carpet. A village pond where frogs still outnumber bicycle frames and tatty bedspreads. A meadow backing onto childhood. A friendly old tree still chuckling at those impish breezes of October, 1987.

Another school of thought attracting some sympathy says we ought to hide the area's biggest lights under a bushel to help stem the flood of folk wanting to move in. The more we sing our own praises, with "God's own acre" and "unspoilt charm" figuring in most verses, the sharper will become pressure for change

The pragmatist says that debate is irrelevant whether it's built on absolute sincerity or just a puckish whim. These are boom times in a boom area. The trend is unstoppable.

The parochial diehard counters emphatically and cleverly with grisly examples from other places where the same creed has been invited to run rampant. Nor can he overlook the irony that several paid-up members of his complaining chorus asked to join after running away from those very places overloaded with concrete and congestion.

A common trait of recent Norfolk years. Last ones in can be first to call for the door to be locked behind them. They know there's bound to be a fresh offensive designed to muck up the very things that had them packing their bags.

I can help by highlighting a few of our shortcomings being overlooked in all the exploitat... sorry, I mean excitement.

For a start, there's no first-class cricket for miles, no chance to see our Test players in action. The natives are at best disdainful, at worst downright hostile. Basic difference lies somewhere between the way they lave double 16 or one, double one when you get accepted after 15 years and invited to team up on the local darts board.

Public transport simply has not recovered from Dr Beeching's rotten medicine and many roads can be blocked for months on end as soon as there's a breath of wind to go with the snow.

Several other little problems.

Like countryside smells and noises, some of them emanating from uncommunicative peasants themselves. Like constant begging-bowl visits from the parson trying to raise money for the nine churches under his umbrella.

Like a postman with an Essex accent asking you where Honeysuckle Cottage is located. Like three dozen people anxious to take up residence on the daisy-decked pastures behind your charming new home.

Comparisons can be melodious, especially in the hands of speculative developers and estate agents armed with a Roget's Thesaurus open at the page with several alternatives to "desirable." However, certain blunt truths must be told.

Already, Norfolk has taken its fair share of The Boot People –The Car Boot People who lift up their lids for a service of thanksgiving every Sunday morning and other nomadic tribes intrigued by the sound of hemlock and parsley growing.

So what prospects now of a good old shake-up on the golden road to Shangri-La? Word of mouth will remain a key component in any "it's not really all it's cracked up to be, you know" campaign.

Volunteers are being sought to yell short but sincere warnings at passport control on the county borders. A modified version of "Abandon hope all ye who enter here" is being prepared. "Look owt!" and "Cleer orff!" are just two suggestions on the table at ACAS (Average Communities' Alarming Suspicions.)

A gospel of gentle persuasion rather than a set of stringent rules .That's the proper Norfolk way

CASH CONTROL

A Norfolk lad came home from school to reveal he'd put down his name for a trip to London.

Grandfather handed him a £10 note, adding: "If yew dunt spend it, let me hev it back!"

The lad returned from his trip.

Grandfather asked if he had any money left

"Yis," replied the boy, "but I spent yar tenner fust!"

NORFOLK VERSES

HEART

Here beats the heart of Norfolk
Around a village pond
Where the silence pushes outwards
And every weed a wand
To conjure up a jungle
For water-hens and toads
Who know this is much safer
Than yonder noisy roads

Here beats the heart of Norfolk
Around a village green
Shy bits-and-pieces nature
Can hide where it has been
The insect congregation
May mime a hymn of praise
But the rabbit's cheeky scamper
Shows far more brazen ways

Here beats the heart of Norfolk
With a clutch of houses neat
Old chimneys nod acquaintance
And the roads still welcome feet
Much more than pretty pictures
And cobwebbed yokel tales
Here beats the heart of Norfolk
Make sure it never fails.

THE FIELD EATERS

Spread out the tablecloth under that old oak tree
And bring your fork and digger
Gorge yourself on a pastoral past

HOW TO SURVIVE IN NORFOLK

And watch the holes grow bigger
Hemlock Avenue and Bramble Drive
Keep the peasants' dreams alive
Peasants old and peasants new
Wait to wash in morning dew

Push back the rusty hurdle and let it loll to bits
While high heels try to scamper
Where the shade is kinder still
And the lid off the hamper
Lupin Lane and Primrose Way
Let the peasants have their say
Peasants old and peasants new
Can always find the morning dew

Pick up the tablecloth and shake out the crumbs
And leave them for tomorrow
When the birds can scavenge
On memories of a furrow
Poppy Place and Ragwort Road
Let the peasants share the load
Peasants old and peasants new
Telling tales of morning dew.

ROADS

Bypass jackboot scuffs and kicks
and blackens green
Dualled dreams die on a hospital
pillow but still
they chisel out slogans for
Roads to Prosperity
Fast-filling acres around reinforce
concrete thinking
And did those diggers in modern times
stalk across Norfolk's
pastures green and
was it wholly glad to nod
and let them mock
a pleasing homely scene?
Economies turn and fashions change

but a road is a road
There is no abridged version

CHANGE

Don't scream
Try sobbing quietly instead
they'll take more notice then
of a left-over
Change came
but you couldn't square it
with the world they
never knew
Your knowledge
is your pain and strength
They can inflict the one
to sham the other
Don't scream
for it gives them marks
they don't deserve
as change comes

NEXT-DOOR JACK

Save the best cakes for Sunday
When the strangers come to tea
Clear up the crumbs on Monday
When there's only you and me

The smiles we kept for next-door Jack
Went crooked when he died
We hung them up down Puffball Track
And watched the chromium tide
Wash over his old flat cap

The broken gate took on new charm
It asked for a family post
They hung it up down Primrose Farm
Where Springtime-sharing grows
And mocks an Autumn past

Next-door Jack still has a part
To play as darkness falls
He hangs around the old Red Hart
To nudge when legend stalls
He sort of sings a song

The tune and words disguise the strain
Of an old man really dead
But told to walk down memory land
With a flat cap on his head
Pied Piper's telling verse

Save the best cakes for Sunday
When the strangers come to tea
Clear up the cups on Monday
When there's only you and me.

END OF SUMMER
(written on a trip to Italy
in September, 1991)

I was homesick in Tuscany when my
boy started school
And I peered through the mists to
see my first days
In a room where tears and smiles
set you up for life

A storm after dark lit up the skies
and brought some rain
To a parched land in September
full of sunflowers
And more tourists wondering if
the path is too worn

"Look up the Brownings for me in Florence!"
smiled an old hand
As we left Norfolk in search
of new treasures

HOW TO SURVIVE IN NORFOLK

In ancient places where they have learnt
to charge for the past

We went to Assisi for the saint
and found trinkets
The birdsong of innocence has long
drifted away
From a playground where the games
are too serious

We went to scorched Rome for the Pope
and his legion
Of pilgrims who had marched
on the Vatican
For a blessing to help ease
the winter journey

We came home to Norfolk in a damp
morning darkness
To look for small churches at the end
of quiet lanes
And an uncluttered faith that has
no need of crowds

COUNTRYMAN

You can't put a farm in a city
Or an office block down my lane
A pitchfork's no good with concrete
And computers don't grow grain
You can bring a dream from the city
And nurture it down my lane
But I can't live in the shadows
Of a tumult that gave you pain
Don't bring your nightmare with you
And let it loose down my lane
Else I'll tell you straight. old partner...
Just you clear orff back again!

BACKWORD
(Norfolk opposite to Foreword)

The Norfolk Yuppy, home-grown or imported, has long been searching for the asparagus kettle in the back of the Golf.

Some pubs are now licensed for Yappies (dog show devotees), Yippees (Country and Western music fanatics) and Tuppies (people who get on your wick at parties.)

There's general condemnation of the Thrummies, the motor-bike brigade revving up and down every village street, and the Tooties, your very own Dukes of Hazard from Top Gear with melodic horns they had for Christmas.

Once you've pushed through the Birmingham Navy on parade in Broadland, you can salute the Yotties and the Yellerwellies around the Burnhams, Blakeney and Brancaster.

But there's a new crew putting down anchor around any duckpond or thatched cottage left behind by the latest wagon train of local estate agents heading for the Home Counties.

Yonders are rather aloof, folk you talk about rather than talk to. A toss of the head can indicate clear water between them and you.

Yelpers are settlers who start moaning ten years later that this isn't a patch on where they came from.

Yearners are natives who wish the Yelpers would put that theory to the test. And take the Yonders with them.

Yawners have heard it raging round them since time immoral.

Yeasties pretend to work themselves into a ferment on behalf of all parties, join the parish council – and mellow into Yawners.

None of these should be confused with the good old Yarner.He sits and fabricates in the pub snug, just your average Norfolk native happy to reflect on the vagaries of lesser mortals.

EPICLOG
(Norfolk answer to the Epilogue)

Ill fares the land, to hastening ills a prey.
Where wealth accumulates and men decay.
Princes and lords may flourish or may fade;
A breath can make them, as a breath has made;
But a bold peasantry, their country's pride,
When once destroyed, can never be supplied.

The Deserted Village (Oliver Goldsmith)

This is the land of lost content,
I see it shining plain;
The happy highways where I went
And cannot come again.

A Shropshire Lad (A E Houseman)

We can't show yew a mount'n.
An' bor, we're short o'hills,
An; yew oon't taake long a-countin'
Ar castles an'ar mills.
But dunt yew sit there sighin'-
Jus' caast yar oyes up high
Where clouds an' baads are flyin',
An' see ar Norfick sky!

Dew Yew Look Up! (John Kett).

APPENDAGE ONE
QUAINT CUSTOMS
(Appendage in Norfolk means a bonus for the readers)

When I was a lad, anniversaries meant a packed Methodist chapel, a visiting preacher with a dinner-plate buttonhole, recitations on crumpled paper behind your back in case of emergency and a handsome collection towards the annual seaside outing.

We had the odd Coronation tea party, Jubilee tea and Thanksgiving supper to mark the end of a war or invasion or the start of a new blackberry-picking campaign.

Generally, though ,we sauntered along as willing hostages to the rolling seasons, calling "hold gee!" at harvest time, "hold hard!" at closing time and wondering why we couldn't find the white snowplough when winter winds blew and cut us off from the rest of the world.

The ancient ritual of dwile-flonking had yet to be invented, ale still being drunk with gratitude rather than being splashed about as if there were no tomorrow.

We had to make our own amusements –hence a penchant for white snowploughs, loosely-tethered goats on the green, inkwells full of frogspawn, collapsible bicycle seats, swivelling signposts to confuse the Vikings and school inspectors and a smoking Tortoise stove to shorten sermons in the chapel.

It was harmless rural fun to complement the regular rhythms of a Norfolk largely at ease with itself. Communities were small and closely-knit, tied to the land and the eternal secrets of overgrown headlands and bountiful hedgerows. Set-aside then was the few shillings you saved and put under the bed for a rainy day.

There was genuine satisfaction in knowing where the fun came from. No question of the wrong person finishing up in the stocks or in the barrel of rotten apples behind the pub.

Times change. Country life has lost much of its spontaneity while demands for it to be revived are on the increase. New villagers, often drawn in the first instance by tales of rustic rituals designed to keep indigenous folk amused before satellite dishes, orienteering, paintballing and real ale, are digging up anniversaries by the barrow-load.

Happenings that used to happen so easily no-one thought them unusual in a particular area now assume a mystique bordering on the supernatural.

Take the traditional Norfolk routine of dickey-dawdling where rival hamlets reflected the virtues of a gentle, more sensitive age by pitting their slowest donkeys against each other on the last Saturday in July.

The animal taking the longest to complete the two-furlong course on neutral territory, while deemed not to have stopped or taken on board any form of sustenance at any stage of the journey, was crowned King Dickey in the first week of August -- if the competition had ended.

There are moves to revive this rural delight in the west of the county, mainly in the hope of making it an Olympic sport in time for the 2028 Games, but using traffic wardens or old-fashioned bicycles in place of perambulating donkeys. Arts Council backing is promised but purists say it simply won't be the same. They have a point.

Norfolk has seen the socially significant and deeply moving Soak the Suffragette manifestation of Edwardian country house gatherings reduced to a garden fete knockabout sideshow called Drench the Wench. So politically incorrect it mocks all progress made in certain departments over the past century and a bit.

We have the brave new custodians of revels, festivals and wakes con-fuse swan-upping at Downham with pint-downing at Upton. We have winced at the questioning of fertility-inducing merits of rolling pork cheeses along disused railway lines. The pre-Beeching era was noted for lack of complaints about the habit.

We know there is reluctance to accept the Dunmow Flitch as a Norfolk custom in origin despite firm evidences it was popular in the thirteenth century as the Dunhame Itch. Married couples resident in either Grete or Littel Dunhame who could prove they had not uttered a civil word to each other during a period of at least seven years and a day after the wedding were given leave to separate, along with a voucher for a side of salted beef.

It all adds up to serious doubts about the amount of due care and attention likely to be paid by those claiming to seek country anchors in a changing world. From well-undressing for hardy maidens and shy bach-elors on January 15th to forelock-tugging for those of a subservient dis-position on any five dates in October, well-loved Norfolk ceremonies must be retained as comfortingly fixed points on the modern calendar.

June 27th, of course, is Dogrose Day when courting couples all over the county rise early to catch the morning on those lovely hedgerow flowers for time-honoured cheek-brushing rites. The beau chants this refrain as his dew-damp fingers caress his loved one's face:
Ask not the reason from whence it did spring,
For you know very well 'tis an old ancient thing.
A ritual unrivalled in its summer simplicity and beauty, although

Suffolk's Ragwort Week, involving retired coalmen and former debutantes from Sudbury, has its supporters.

However, if you want to participate in a real winter warmer which still perplexes multitudes of Norfolk newcomers, I recommend a practice set deep in pagan soil.

A dank November day with rain, wind, fog, frost and mud round the edges is an ideal setting for Beeting the Raretreat. To renew vows to Mother Earth (and local branch of the National Union of Agricultural Workers) wear a tattered cap, collarless shirt, open waistcoat, overalls with sacking tied to the knees with binder twine, hobnailed boots without laces and a smile that looks genuine.

Select two items on either side from a large root crop and bang them together to banish dark underground forces. Place them neatly in lines for your following companion, male or female, to defoliate with one swish of a sharp hook to signify the frailty of Mother Earth's children.

At the end of each row, after a swig of cold tea from a bottle and a glance at dark skies above, both participants bow, turn and prepare for fresh action with the incantation:

Come, guard the bounty, for us there's no stoppin'
It's bewtiful weather for knockin' and toppin'

Norfolk can ill afford to surrender such fertile ground.

LONG INNINGS

A visitor to a remote Norfolk railway station many years ago noticed it was deserted except for the stationmaster and porter.

They were playing cricket. Try as he would, the porter simply could not take the wicket of the stationmaster. The visitor picked up the ball, sent down a fast one... and the innings ended abruptly.

Grasping him warmly by the hand, the porter said: "Cor, blarst, I ent harf glad yew dun that. He're bin in fer four years."

APPENDAGE TWO
SQUIT PARTY

One of Spike Milligan's favourite yarns concerns a young man who lied about his height to get into the police force. A good trick if you can manage it, although suspicion remains it is nothing more than a tall story invented and then spread by the Goons.

Even so, it may help put into perspective some remarkable allegations aimed at towering figures heading the recently-formed Norfolk Squit Party – Stop Quangos Undermining Indigenous Traditions.

The inspirational pair is Hadrian Mule (aged 97?), a semi-retired dialect coach from Stow Bedon, and Bolshie Billhook, 93, a still-active snake charmer from East Lexham with a second home on Litcham Common. It is a measure of their spirited resistance to the threat of rampant regionalism that they have been singled out for a vitriolic attack from "faceless biro-crats" in Bedford, Cambridge, Chelmsford, Milton Keynes and Braintree.

These pillars of Norfolk society, battling for autonomy in an increasingly centralised world, stand accused of "exaggerating their years to give them a veneer of venerability in pursuit of a doomed cause."

They are being dismissed as "bucolic leftovers from a village pantomime somewhere in darkest Norfolk" and "small-minded relics of a drawbridge generation who left the county gasping for progress."

Response has been predictably loud and direct. Hadrian Mule brandished "buth susstificates" to prove they are not fibbing about their ages. Bolshie Billhook decreed on his website, homeruleforNorfolk.com, that "growin' owld is mandertory, but growin' up is opshunal."

He also points out there is nothing exceptional about folk over 90 being at the sharp end of important matters in his home county.. "Blarst, some plearces 'long the Norfolk coast we'd be towld we're still damp ahind the lugs"

His colleague added:" My ole Uncle Walter lived ter be 107 an' he owed it all ter mushrooms. He never et'em."

This Norfolk home guard, cheered rather than chastened by insults from faraway places, now seeks a mandate from true natives and enlightened newcomers to take the fight into enemy territory. A mystery outing to St Neots is being organised by the Stow Bedon Charabanc Company, Foreign Travel Dept., and a fact-finding tour of Huntingdon is on the cards. If John Major is able to act as interpreter.
The Squit Party is on the march!

APPENDAGE THREE
DIALECT BOOKS

Books written about and in the Norfolk dialect remain popular, although several have long been out of print. A hunt round local second-hand book shops can usually bring dividends.

Here's a list of recommended reading, including the poems of John Kett and Bible stories written in the Norfolk dialect by Colin Riches.

Michael Brindid: "I Din't Say Nothin'!" Norfolk dialect letters to the *Eastern Daily Press*, 1995. "I Din't Say Nothin' Ag'in!" 1998, both published by M. Brindid and produced by Jim Baldwin, Fakenham

"Broad Norfolk": being a series of articles and letters reprinted from the *Eastern Daily Press*. Published 1893 by Norfolk News Co. Norwich, editor Harry Cozens-Hardy.

Tony Clarke: *Mighta Bin Wuss; Tales of the Boy Jimma*, Nostalgia Publications, 1998. *Thass A Rum Ow Job, more tales of the Boy Jimma*, Nostalgia Publications, 1999.

W.N.Dew: *A Dyshe of Norfolk Dumplings*. First published in 1898 by Jarrold Publishers. Republished 1973.

Ida Fenn: *Tales of a Countryman* – stories of the Boy Jimma in Norfolk dialect. Published 1973 by Reeve, Wymondham.

Robert Forby: *The Vocabulary of East Anglia*. Two volumes originally published in 1830. Reprinted 1970 by Latimer Trend & Co. Ltd.

Eric Fowler (who wrote under the pseudonym of Jonathan Mardle): *Broad Norfolk*, written by the Readers of the *Eastern Daily Press*, January 21 – March 19, 1949. *Broad Norfolk*, published in 1973 by Wensum Books of Norwich.

Edward Gillett: *The Song of Solomon in the Norfolk Dialect*. From the authorised English Version. First printed 1861, published 1862 by Thew, King's Lynn. Republished 1993 by Larks Press, Guist Bottom, East Dereham.

Sidney Grapes: *The Boy John Letters*. First published in volume form by Norfolk News Co. 1958. Published by Wensum Books, 1974. A fresh delivery from Mousehold Press, 2003 with introduction by Keith Skipper. Also a CD in which Keith reads 12 of the Boy John Letters.

Lilias Rider Haggard edited *I Walked By Night, Being the Life and History of the King of the Norfolk Poachers*. First published in 1935 by Nicholson and Watson, London. She also edited *The Rabbit Skin Cap*, a tale of a Norfolk countryman's youth. First published 1939. Reprinted by the Norfolk Library, 1974, 1975, 1976.

John Kett: four volumes of dialect poems – *Tha's a Rum'un, Bor*, 1973. *Tha's a Rum'un Tew*, published 1973 by Baron Publishing, Woodbridge, *Watcher Bor*, published by Wensum Books, 1979 and *A Late Lark Singing*, published by Minerva Press, 1997.

Robert Malster: *The Mardler's Companion, a Dictionary of East Anglian Dialect*, Malthouse Press, 1999.

Mary Mann: *The Fields of Dulditch*, first published in 1902. Reissued 1976 by Boydell Press, Ipswich. *Tales of Victorian Norfolk*, published by Morrow and Co., Bungay, 1991

John Greaves Nall: *Glossary of the Dialect and Provincialisms of East Anglia*, originally published in 1866 by Longmans, Green, Reeder and Dyer, London. Republished by Larks Press, 2006

Old Barney: A series of broadcasts on BBC Radio Norfolk in three volumes edited by Keith Skipper – *Dew Yew Keep a'Troshin'*, 1984, *Down at the Datty Duck*, 1985, and *Dunt Fergit Ter Hevver Larf*, 1986. All published by Jim Baldwin, Fakenham.

Colin Riches: Bible stories in the Norfolk dialect, *Dew Yew Lissen Hare*, published 1975 by George Nobbs Publishing; *Orl Bewtiful an' New*, published 1978 by F. Crowe & Sons Ltd, Norwich.

Walter Rye: *Glossary of Words Used in East Anglia*, published 1895 for the English Dialect Society by Henry Frowde, Oxford University Press.

Keith Skipper: *The Norfolk Companion*, Jim Baldwin Publishing, 1994. *Larn Yarself Norfolk, a Comprehensive Guide to the Norfolk Dialect*,

Nostalgia Publications, 1996. *Hev Yew Gotta Loight, Boy?* the life and lyrics of Allan Smethurst, The Singing Postman, Countryside Books, 2001

James Spilling: *Giles' Trip to London*, first published by Jarrold Publishing, 1872. Facsimile edition in 1998.

Peter Trudgill: *The Norfolk Dialect*, Poppyland Publishing, 2003

B. Knyvet Wilson: *Norfolk Tales and Memories*, published 1930. *More Norfolk Tales and Memories*, 1931, both published by Jarrold and Sons Ltd.

Arnold Wesker: *The Wesker Trilogy*, including *Roots* (set in Norfolk) published 1984 by Penguin Books Ltd, Harmondsworth, Middlesex.

There are many dialect articles to be culled from old copies of both the *Norfolk Magazine* and the *East Anglian Magazine*. Again, these can often be picked up in second-hand book shops.

BLANK LOOKS

A smart city motorist pulled up at Weybourne and asked the way to Blakeney.

"There's a signpost harf a mile down the rud," replied the local inhabitant.

The motorist, in a teasing mood, said he couldn't read.

"Well, that sign'll suit yew then," added the local. "There ent noffin' onnit."

APPENDAGE FOUR
MY TOP TWENTY

I am often asked to come up with a recommended reading list for those who would know more about Norfolk. A flattering invitation – but a nigh-impossible task as books are so much about highly personal tastes.

As journalist, author, broadcaster and arch-parochialist for well over 40 years, I have devoured countless home-grown volumes and held on to quite a few of them. I turn regularly for solace and sustenance to favourite authors who have become old friends over the years.

With dialect offerings already lined up for inspection, I now take the big risk of placing certain other Norfolk delights ahead of hundreds of others on my shelves. It is at once a painful exercise and a rewarding experience... sad to leave so many quality items out of the spotlight but heartening to consider the sheer class of a chosen few.

I whittled a short-list of about 250 down to a score for the sake of this exercise, urging my selections forward as a genuine incentive to sample and savour, catch the true Norfolk spirit and then move on to find regular companions of your own. Several of my suggestions are long out of print but visits to the local library or closest second-hand bookshop can reap happy little harvest. Here's my top 20 in no particular order of merit:

Arthur Mee's *Norfolk, Green Pastures and Still Waters,* was first published in the King's England series by Hodder & Stoughton in 1940 with a distinct whiff of wartime patriotism. It remains a compulsive chronicle with nearly 200 photographs to underline what the county has surrendered since – and what glories remain to be cherished.

With coastal erosion and rising sea levels constant topics for concern in a county all but surrounded by water, **Dorothy Summers'** *The East Coast Floods* (David & Charles, 1978) continues to serve as a powerful warning. She concentrates on the great disaster of 1953, wondering if certain harsh lessons will ever be learnt.

A rousing history of the farmworkers' battle to rise above grinding poverty is told in *Sharpen The Sickle,* by **Reg Groves**. First published in 1949 by the Porcupine Press, it was given fresh life by the Merlin Press in 1981 as a massive drift from the land intensified. Norfolk's role in rural trade unionism, with George Edwards to the fore, is a proud one.

Cyril Jolly (I knew him well as Methodist preacher and fine writer) went through choppy waters to pen and publish his biography of *Henry Blogg of Cromer, Greatest of the Lifeboatmen,* in 1958. Blogg was a very private man and said little, but this remains a richly-praised account of "one of the bravest men who lived."

For sustained humour with that full Norfolk flavour, it is hard to beat *Prewd and Prejudice.* **Chris Sugden** and **Sid Kipper**, an inseparable pair, put this rural epic together for the Mousehold Press in 1994. The laughs are still flowing as Miss Prewd offers her 1904 reflections of life in St Just-near-Trunch after leaving the rarefied air of polite London society. Plenty for newcomers to ponder here...

I interviewed **Professor AJ Ayer** on BBC Radio Norfolk's Dinnertime Show in March 1988 about his new book on one of Norfolk's most influential sons. His *Thomas Paine* (Secker & Warburg) remains for me the definitive look at the bright lad from Thetford who went on to deal with the great issues of any age. And his father made corsets.

Clement Scott's *Poppyland*, first published in 1886 and reprinted just over a century later as a facsimile of the original, is much more than a flowery evocation of an area near Cromer destined to become a highly fashion able part of the tourists' playground. It serves as a potent reminder of what can happen to quiet places if the advertising is up top scratch. Essential fare for all visitors before they go to Burnham Market.

Fenland's leading ambassador for many years before moving to find a different perspective in Wales, **Edward Storey** remains a close friend and inspiration. His *Spirit of The Fens,* published by Robert Hale in 1985 with a foreword by Graham Swift of *Waterland* fame, is a collection of essays, reflections and interviews admirably summing up his qualities as a poetic writer about a world revelling in its differences.

Robert Wyndham Ketton-Cremer lived in historic splendour at Felbrigg Hall near Cromer before he left it to the National Trust. He died in 1969, the year in which his classic *Norfolk in the Civil War* was first published. It was reissued by Gliddon Books in 1985 and continues to impress all kinds of scholars anxious to know how the old county reacted to the ferment of the 1640s.

Dedicated "to all who have worked and suffered for the land and the people of Greater Britain", *The Story of a Norfolk Farm* is **Henry**

Williamson's account of how the dreamer came face to face with harsh reality on the eve of the Second World War. He had to learn how to work the land as he ploughed his own highly individual furrows on moving from Devon to the North Norfolk coast. A controversial figure with right-wing inclinations – but no doubts about his literary talents.

Juicy Joe, A Romance of the Norfolk Marshlands, first published in 1903 by Grant Richards, is the idea antidote to any lingering "good old days" notions about rural existence at the end of the Victorian era. **James Blyth** spared no feelings in this remarkable novel and the stinging preface introducing his colourful cast makes Jeremy Clarkson seem like a good friend to Norfolk. A real image-buster of a book.

The doughty **Lucilla Reeve**, cast simply as "A Norfolk Woman" on the title page, tilled *The Earth No Longer Bare* out of her experiences as a Breckland farmer during the Second World War. This engrossing little book, published by George Reeve of Wymondham, underlines her resilience and purpose in trying to tame unforgiving soil while the machinery of war rattled her hedges and gates.

Arthur Patterson wrote under the gloriously self-effacing pseudonym of John Knowlittle. An outstanding naturalist from Yarmouth, he travelled *Through Broadland in a Breydon Punt* just after the First World War, providing sketches and photographs for the inevitable book to follow. It is a compelling dip into yesterday's more tranquil waters for any who want to feel what Broadland used to be like.

Definitely one of the books I'd take to my desert island, **Lilias Rider Haggard**'s *Norfolk Notebook,* first published in 1946, deals with local life in years leading up to war. For all the uncertainties of the 1930s, it is a volume rich in proper rural values and genuine optimism for the future of country dwellers. Wonderful descriptive powers make Lilias a winner for all seasons – and all eras.

Of course, her father **Henry Rider Haggard** was a useful scribe as well. *A Farmer's Year* is his diary of 1898 when he farmed 350 acres at Bedingham and Ditchingham. Republished in 1987 by the Cresset Library with a foreword by countryside champion Ronald "Akenfield" Blythe, it is now regarded as essential reading for anyone who wants to know how and why the rural scene we size up today has emerged.

Voted by many as the most gifted sportsman to come out of Norfolk, Bill

Edrich showed exceptional courage both as international cricketer and wartime pilot. His biography by **Alan Hill**, published by Andre Deutsch in 1994, gives full rein to a run-spattered career with Middlesex and England before he returned to his native pitch to captain Norfolk for a dozen memorable years. His devil-may-care lifestyle may not fall easily into the typical Norfolk mould, but W.J. Edrich batted at a different crease to most.

The **Rev Benjamin Armstrong**, Vicar of East Dereham from 1850 until 1888, kept a comprehensive diary of his years in and around the parish. Edited by his grandson, it was first published by George Harrap & Co in 1949 to wide acclaim. A second volume followed in 1963, although the cream of the crop had already been harvested. With plenty of dry humour and scathing comments, *A Norfolk Diary* throws fascinating light on Victorian life in this neck of the wood.

Norfolk's geography meant it had no less than 37 airfields by the end of the Second World War. All come under scrutiny in **Graham Smith**'s impeccably researched history published by Countryside Books in 1994. *Norfolk Airfields in the Second World War* also reveals what is left for enthusiasts who go in search of ghosts down old runways.

No Halt At Sunset, the diary of a country housewife by **Elizabeth Harland**, first saw light of day in 1951, Festival of Britain Year, and was then reissued by the Boydell Press in 1974. It does exactly what it says on the cover, and there are loads of recipes and household hints from an age when austerity spelt invention. Plenty of chuckles and sideways glances.

The ideal answer for those who still cry for more... *Literary Norfolk,* by **Julian Earwaker** and **Kathleen Becker**, with a foreword by the king of creative writing Malcolm Bradbury. This glorious companion (Chapter 6 Publishing, Ipswich, 1998) embraces more than 150 authors spanning seven centuries through landscapes real and imagined. A literary pilgrimage to relish and an indispensable guide.

APPENDAGE FIVE
WORD GAMES

It started when the chap on the farm called the new mechanical monster a concubine harvester. We said he drove erotically and gave him free electrocution lessons.

Then a local Methodist preacher told us Moses collected the Ten Commandments on Mount Cyanide. And we think he said Salome danced in front of Harrods.

A boy in my class at grammar school definitely wrote Ali Baba is saying that you were somewhere else when you were there –and proving it. Only the other day I heard an old Norfolk worthy suggest a lot of people go to Walsingham where they throw that incest about.

Rustic malapropisms, schoolboy groaners, family foibles (or at least the ones Aesop didn't use), tips of the slongue and priceless Norfolkisms ... I have collected a big crop over the years.

I know Walter Gabriel's old granny used to come out with some rum sayings and every Norfolk village must have had her equivalent when I was a lad. They were at their best when describing ailments, ranging from haricot veins to multiplication of the bowels.

"They reckon our blood's med up o' tew kind's o'corkscrews – red corkscrews and white 'uns "and "She had ter hev sum o'them, contradictive pills" still make me chortle. As does the famous notice in a country doctor's surgery:" No torkin' – an' hev yar simptums riddy."

There was nothing medical about the ceremony as far as I know, but many a new Norfolk vicar was induced before being told what time to celebrate Holy Commotion. The old churchwarden had the perfect answer when asked by a newcomer if they had matins in the church: "No, ole partner, we hev lino ryte up ter the altar."

The village shop was another rich source of instant humour, some of it off the top shelf reserved for regular packages. Old Harry only once had to ask for a roll of Anthrax and a legend was born. Martha's girl needed but a single order for some of that Coronation Milk to go on tinned peaches and her place in local folklore was assured. Young Walter would be destined for stardom as soon as he admitted to listening to the fizz of them Helter Skelter tablets in the glass.

Several rounds of chuckling down at The Truculent Tractor as one regular said he was ready to throw his hat into the political marina as soon as they called local election time and another urged all right-minded customers to sign his partition against them tricolated lorries thundering through the parish.

Landlord joins in the spirit by asking who wants to see the holiday snaps he took in Essex with a new Paranoid camera while his wife wonders if the Morris dancers calling next week might reveal the secrets of their futility rites.

I recall an old salt at Gorleston listening for one of them macaroons to launch the lifeboat. I heard a dear old girl at Yarmouth describe how those indecency bombs had scared her witless during the war. I noted how a Caister fisherman was convinced herrings went about the sea in shawls.

A Fakenham man told me he had seen a real Lord wearing a scarlet robe trimmed with vermin. When his wife got excited – that's the Fakenham man who could paint wonderful pictures with words –she was overcome with emulsion. Probably to the extent of going into a shop to ask for a pint of semi-skilled milk.

Little blasts from notebooks past. And I'm still jotting down little gems. Like the woman who always got her facts and names slightly muddled. "Didn't Stanley Matthews marry one of them Andrews Sisters? Tell you my favourite film star... that Eddie Nelson. They asked me if I liked Delius. I told 'em ... got all her recipes."

There's more fun to be had with comparatively new words. Many a Norfolk computer travels into the city for work each day. I was reliably informed that an 87-year-old retired farm worker, yet to surf the Internet, had started a villaganti movement. I approached with caution. He told me it was quite simple. He lived in the village where he was born. He was anti newcomers.

Then there's this classic from the Norfolk village classroom.

The teacher explained that "excavate" meant "to hollow out." She asked for a sentence using "excavate". Up shot Charlie's hand.

"Please, miss. I know. I dropped a big ole weight on my Dad's toe an' he excavated."

APPENDAGE SIX
LITTE GEMS

Norfolk has got used to being insulted, often by two-bit "celebrities" or unfunny comedians settling for stock targets. I sense that most of the adverse comments are born out of sheer envy or simple frustration at being ignored by people of equitable temperament and superior intelligence.

If a reasonable debate about the county's merits or otherwise does take shape, it's good to have a few uplifting quotes to back the home case. Happily, I can provide a host of little gems collected to bring sunshine to rainy days. Take your pick and use wisely:

"The Norfolk people are very quick and smart in their motions and in their speaking. Very neat and trim in all their farming concerns and very skilful. Great admiration for this county of excellent farmers and hearty, open and spirited men." – **William Cobbett, 1821**.

"A solid man. Lots of beef and beer, tempered with the east wind, have gone to the making of him. Once he is sure you are not going to cheat him or be very grand and affected he is a friendly chap; but if you want the other thing you can have it. Perhaps we of the West Riding brought some of our aggressive qualities from Norfolk." - **JB Priestley, 1933**.

"Let any stranger find me out so pleasant a county, such good ways, large heaths, three such places as Norwich, Yarmouth and Lynn in any county in England, and I'll be once again a vagabond and visit them." – **Sir Thomas Browne, seventeenth century**.

"For the traveller in search of the English heritage, this county is a paradise. It has great cliffs and chalk downs, a history far older than any written documents, delightful rivers, unique still waters, low-lying fens, captivating towns, a historic roll of famous folk and a group of Saxon, Norman and medieval churches crammed with the beauty that makes England the matchless country of the world." – **Arthur Mee, 1940**.

"If the rest of Britain sank beneath the waves, and Norfolk was left alone, islanded in the turmoil of the seas, it would, I think, survive without too much trouble ...Norfolk has always stood alone and aloof from the rest of England." – **James Wentworth Day, 1976**.

"Why go to the Alps or hanker after the Mediterranean or think of Germany –pshaw! – when a sort of Eden by the Yare winds round the bends." – **Arthur Patterson, 1920.**

"Norfolk would not be Norfolk without a church tower on the horizon or round a corner up the lane. We cannot spare a single Norfolk church. When a church has been pulled down the country seems empty or is like a necklace with a jewel missing." – **John Betjeman, 1972.**

"The great piece of husbandry in which Norfolk excels is in the management of turnips, from which it derives an inestimable advantage." – **Nathaniel Kent, 1796.**

"It was the least changed part of old England, with only a few visitors in summer. This was attractive to me after the Devon coast, which had changed so rapidly since I had known it, becoming built upon and populous." – **Henry Williamson, 1941.**

"Yarmouth, the paradise of excursionists... one scarcely knows how to take it, so to say, whether to look upon it as the haunt pure and simple of the cheap 'tripper' or to regard it as a quaint old seaport, picturesque in the highest degree, interesting from end to end; a place wherein to study the old' salt' in his native lair, or to take 'impressions' of the East –end holidaymaker in his most festive mood." – **Annie Berlyn, 1894.**

"Never be ashamed of the customs of good old Norfolk. If we are behind the times compared with other counties, we can console ourselves with the thought that Norfolk men have played their part, and that right well, in the stirring events of our nation's history" – **Walton N Dew, 1896.**

"Norfolk is still one of the most beautiful counties in England and has probably been able to hang on to its real character longer than most because of its geographical position. When I talk to people who have known the county more years than I can remember they tell me that I have already missed the best, that times have changed very much since the war and the atmosphere of the place is not anything like as quiet as it used to be." – **Edward Storey, 1978.**

"All England may be carved out of Norfolk, represented therein not only to the kind but degree itself. Here are fens and heaths, and light and deep, and sand and clay ground, and meadows and pastures, and arable and woody, and (generally) woodless land; so grateful is this shire with the variety thereof. Thus, as in many men, through perchance this or that part, may justly be cavilled at, yet all put together complete a proper person; so Norfolk, collectively taken, hath a sufficient result of pleasure and profit, that being supplied in one part, which, is defective in another." – **Thomas Fuller, 1662.**

"The only trouble about motoring through Norfolk is that however slowly you go (and even in Norfolk other drivers get impatient if you hesitate), marvels flash you by." – **Paul Jennings, 1986.**

"It is a privilege to be able to stroll through these lanes or on the salt-marshes or along the river valleys, with the quietness all around and that huge open sky above. Even in the winter when the fields are bleak and the wind is bitter, somehow the world seems a gentler, a calmer, and a more civilised place." – **John Timpson, 1990.**

"Though it has no stupendous mountains furnishing traits of the grand, and no bold and towering cliffs, except a few washed by the ocean, there are many exceptions to the prevailing uniformity of its appearance, particularly in the northern parts, where the general surface is broken into moderate elevations and depressions, where turf-clad hill and fertile valleys are diversified by woods , plantations, hedgerows and other enlivening sylvan decorations, combining all the softer beauties of nature." – **William White, 1845.**

"If our authentic East Anglian rural scenery – our common heritage – is lost, not only will those who love beauty as a sure escape from the ugliness of life suffer, but the whole vast network of business interests who cater, directly or indirectly, for summer visitors and tourist traffic will slowly but surely reap the unpleasant reward of their indifference." – **Lilias Rider Haggard, 1943.**

SADLY MISSED

Two old Norfolk boys had just paid their last respects to a village character.

"Hew yew noticed how the allus say nice things 'bowt people at thar fewnruls?" mused Horry. "Yis," said Bert, "that mearke me sad I'm a'gorn ter miss mine by jist a few days."